Salem

David Calcutt

OXFORD
UNIVERSITY PRESS

OXFORD
UNIVERSITY PRESS

Great Clarendon Street, Oxford OX2 6DP

Oxford University Press is a department of the University of Oxford.
It furthers the University's objective of excellence in research,
scholarship, and education by publishing worldwide in

Oxford   New York

Auckland   Cape Town   Dar es Salaam   Hong Kong   Karachi
Kuala Lumpur   Madrid   Melbourne   Mexico City   Nairobi
New Delhi   Shanghai   Taipei   Toronto

With offices in

Argentina   Austria   Brazil   Chile   Czech Republic   France   Greece
Guatemala   Hungary   Italy   Japan   Poland   Portugal   Singapore
South Korea   Switzerland   Thailand   Turkey   Ukraine   Vietnam

Oxford is a registered trade mark of Oxford University Press
in the UK and in certain other countries

British Library Cataloguing in Publication Data

Data available

ISBN 978 0 19 832103 3

10 9 8 7

Typeset by Palimpsest Book Production Ltd, Grangemouth, Stirlingshire.
Printed and bound by Bell and Bain Ltd, Glasgow.

Acknowledgements

Cover Imagery is courtesy of Corbis UK Ltd.

Artwork is by Donald Harley/B J Kearley Ltd.

The Publisher would like to thank Jenny Roberts for writing the Activity section.

Contents

SALEM CONTENTS

General Introduction

With a fresh, modern look, this classroom-friendly series boasts an exciting range of authors – from Pratchett to Chaucer – whose works have been expertly adapted by such well-known and popular writers as Philip Pullman and David Calcutt.

Many teachers use OXFORD *Playscripts* to study the format, style, and structure of playscripts with their students; for speaking and listening assignments; to initiate discussion of relevant issues in class; to cover Drama as part of the curriculum; as an introduction to the novel of the same title; and to introduce the less able or willing to pre-1914 literature.

At the back of each OXFORD *Playscript*, you will find a brand new Activity section, which not only addresses the points above, but also features close text analysis, and activities that provide support for underachieving readers and act as a springboard for personal writing.

Many schools will simply read through the play in class with no staging at all, and the Activity sections have been written with this in mind, with individual activities ranging from debates and designing campaign posters to writing extra scenes or converting parts of the original novels into playscript form.

For those of you, however, who do wish to take to the stage, each OXFORD *Playscript* also features 'A Note on Staging' – a section dedicated to suggesting ways of staging the play, as well as examining the props and sets you may wish to use.

Above all, we hope you will enjoy using OXFORD *Playscripts*, be it on the stage or in the classroom.

What the Author Says

Any writer of an imaginative work based on historical events is presented with a dilemma: how closely to keep to what actually happened, and how much to change, compress, and even disregard for the sake of artistic or dramatic effect.

Of course, people are constantly making a fiction of the past. If, for example, we have a conversation with someone and they tell us something important, it's the important thing we remember, not the whole conversation. Or when we relate some incident that has happened to us, we tell it in such a way as to give the story form and shape: a beginning, a middle and an end. It's storytelling, and we all do it.

The same thing happens when you write a play based on historical events. It's the things you feel are important that you want to communicate, and you want to place them within a dramatic structure. You want the audience to feel what it was like to be those characters living through those events.

So, when I began to research the Salem Witch Trials for this play, I was looking for facts and events that could be put together to tell some kind of dramatic story. But not only that. I wanted to find a way of coming close to the truth of what happened during that startling episode in human history.

The main sources for my research were two books – *A Delusion of Satan* and *The Salem Witch Trials Reader*, both by Frances Hill. One of the things that struck me about the books was the use made of documentary evidence from the period – eyewitness accounts, journals, transcripts of court hearings, and so on. Reading these was like hearing the voices of those involved speaking directly to me, and I decided that I wanted to try to capture that impression in the play. I wanted some of the chief participants in the events to speak directly to the audience.

One of the characters I especially wanted to speak out to the audience was Tituba, the Parris family's slave. It was she who was first accused of witchcraft by the girls, and who then went on to accuse others. The fact that she was an Indian is probably crucial in understanding how the hysteria that led to the accusations began. The Puritan settlers had a real fear of the native Indians and equated them with devils and demons. It was this climate of fear in Salem that I wanted to portray in the play; and I also wanted to give what the villagers feared a voice. So Tituba speaks, and tells her part of the story.

But it wasn't only the Indians that the Puritans feared. Their own particularly harsh and oppressive religion fed their fears, teaching them that the world was filled with devils and demons. It generated in their minds an almost pathological dread and terror of the world itself. I wanted to find a voice for this too, and this led me to invent a number of scenes that didn't actually happen. The meeting between Elizabeth Parris and Abigail Hobbs is one of these, and there are others. They aren't episodes verifiable by historical research. They are a dramatic way of illustrating what I believe was one of the truths at the heart of the story.

The hysteria began with the girls in Parris's house, but it spread very quickly throughout the whole community. While some may have used it as a means of settling scores with rivals, I'm pretty sure that some of the accusers and witnesses actually believed, or half-believed, the fantastic claims they made at the hearings. The community was plunged into a kind of paranoid nightmare. I wanted to depict this in the play, and came up with the idea of using a Chorus to articulate it.

Sometimes I put words I came across during my research into the mouths of characters who didn't say them. The speeches about the horrors witnessed by Abigail Williams and Mercy Lewis are in fact taken from the accounts of people living in other villages in the area. But it's likely that the girls witnessed something like it. This is an example of the method I used throughout the writing of the play – treating historical research as raw material from which to shape the dramatic narrative.

And that's what this play *Salem* is – a dramatic narrative. It is an imagined version of a story that has been told before and, without doubt, will be told in different ways again and again.

David Calcutt

A Note on Staging

The action of the play covers the years 1689 to 1692, from Samuel Parris's appointment as minister of Salem Village to the start of the witch trials.

The Stage

Scenes are:
Gallows Hill
Salem Village centre
Inside the meeting house
Outside the meeting house
Inside Parris's house
The woods
Inside the gaol

Costumes and Props

Items you may need include:

Samuel Parris	Long black coat; carries a Bible
Sarah Good	Ragged clothes
Dorcas Good	Ragged clothes
Abigail Hobbs	Slightly eccentric, poor quality clothes

Props required in specific scenes

Prologue	Raised area, with steps or a ladder leading up to it. Gallows on the raised area, with a noose hanging from it. Length of rope.
Act 1	
Scene 1	Luggage holding belongings of Parris family; one case strong enough for Elizabeth to sit on.
Scene 2	Set of keys for minister's house
Scene 5	Apple
Scene 8	Letter
Act 2	
Scene 1	A crust of bread
Scene 4	Four homemade dolls, a long, sharp pin
Scene 5	A candle, matches, a glass, a jug of water, an egg

Characters

Chorus — inhabitants of Salem Village

Samuel Parris — Minister of Salem Village from 1689 to 1697

Elizabeth Parris — Samuel Parris's wife, died a few years after the witch trials, in 1696

Tituba — the Parrises' Indian slave, from Barbados

Villagers who support the new Minister and his church

Thomas Putnam — landowner and important member of the Salem Village community

Jonathan Walcott — farmer in Salem Village, married to Thomas Putnam's sister, and close neighbour of Samuel Parris

John Hathorne — merchant and magistrate

Nicholas Noyes — merchant and magistrate

Jonathan Corwin — merchant and magistrate

Villagers who oppose the new Minister and his church

Joseph Putnam — Thomas Putnam's half-brother, to whom their father left all his estate

Isaac Easty — inhabitant of Topsfield, near Salem Village, and opposed to Thomas Putnam and Samuel Parris

Francis Nurse — inhabitant of Topsfield, near Salem Village, and opposed to Thomas Putnam and Samuel Parris

Peter Cloyce — inhabitant of Topsfield, near Salem Village, and opposed to Thomas Putnam and Samuel Parris

The girl accusers

Betty Parris — daughter of Samuel and Elizabeth, nine years old in 1692 when the witch trials began

Abigail Williams — niece of Samuel and Elizabeth, eleven years old in 1692 when the witch trials began

Ann Putnam — daughter of Thomas Putnam, twelve years old in 1692 when the witch trials began

Mercy Lewis — servant to Thomas Putnam, seventeen years old in 1692 when the witch trials began. At the age of fourteen she witnessed the murder of her parents by Indians.

Mary Walcott daughter of Jonathan Walcott, seventeen years old in 1692 when the witch trials began

Mary Warren servant to John and Elizabeth Proctor, twenty years old in 1692 when the witch trials began

the accused

Sarah Good a beggar in Salem Village. Her father had been prosperous but had drowned himself, and she had been cheated of her inheritance by her stepfather. She was married to a wastrel and was the mother of several young children. She was renowned for her bad temper. Imprisoned, tried and hanged 1692 (unnamed infant died in prison).

Dorcas Good one of Sarah Good's children. A young child, she was accused with her mother of witchcraft and imprisoned. The months she spent in prison sent her insane. Imprisoned 1692. Later released, but had lost her mind. Rendered mentally incapable for the rest of her life. (Actual age at the time of her imprisonment was four years old.)

Abigail Hobbs a rebellious girl, daughter of a labouring family living in Topsfield. She frequently wandered alone in the woods at night and slept out of doors. Aged twenty-two in 1692 when the witch trials began. Imprisoned 1692. Became an accuser and was later released.

Mary Easty wife of Isaac Easty, sister of Rebecca Nurse and Sarah Cloyce. The father of the three sisters, Jacob Towne, had a long-standing feud over ownership of land with John Putnam, Thomas Putnam's father. Imprisoned, tried and hanged 1692.

Sarah Cloyce wife of Peter Cloyce, sister of Rebecca Nurse and Mary Easty. Imprisoned 1692, but was never brought to trial and was later released.

Rebecca Nurse wife of Francis Nurse, sister of Mary Easty and Sarah Cloyce. Imprisoned and hanged 1692.

John Proctor Inhabitant of Salem Village, farmer, businessman, tavern-keeper. Aged 60 at the time of the trials. Outspoken critic of the witch-trials. Imprisoned, tried and hanged 1692.

Officials and minor characters

Sheriff
Sheriff's Assistant
Hangman
Carriers
Witnesses

Prologue

*A simple, bare stage. A little to the right of the centre of the stage is a raised area, with either steps or a ladder leading up to it. Above the raised area hangs a noose. The play opens with a single light rising slowly to illuminate the noose. The rest of the stage is in darkness. The **Chorus** of villagers enter. Leading them are the magistrates, **John Hathorne** and **Nicholas Noyes**. Between and in front of them walks **Sarah Good**. She is dressed in rags, and her hands are tied in front of her with a rope. The other end of the rope is held by the **Hangman**, who leads **Sarah**. As the **Chorus** enter, all, except **Sarah**, are chanting softly.*

Chorus   Hang her, hang the witch! Hang her, hang the witch! Hang her, hang the witch! ... *etc.*

*The chanting continues as the lights rise to fill the stage. The **Chorus** gather around the gallows. The **Hangman** leads **Sarah Good** up the steps and places her in front of the noose. All this time, the chanting is growing louder and more insistent.*

Hang her, hang the witch! Hang her, hang the witch! Hang her, hang the witch! ... *etc.*

*Suddenly, **Mary Warren** cries out from the **Chorus**.*

Mary Warren   No!

*Her cry silences the **Chorus**. She runs forward to the steps of the gallows and looks up at **Sarah Good**.*

No.

*She turns to the **Chorus**.*

No more. Let it finish now.

She falls to her knees, clasps her hands, bows her head in prayer.

Chorus   This is Mary Warren
And this is her dream
Her dream and her nightmare
From which she can't wake.

Samuel Parris steps out of the Chorus.

Samuel Parris	There are devils among us.
Chorus	And it's his dream too Samuel Parris, Minister of Salem.
Samuel Parris	Devils as well as saints in Christ's church.
Chorus	The nightmare that plagues him Sleeping and waking.
Samuel Parris	Christ knows who they are, these devils in our midst.

Putnam steps forward from the Chorus.

Thomas Putnam	And we shall not rest until they're rooted out.
Chorus	And his, Thomas Putnam, Farmer, landowner A voice in the village.
Thomas Putnam	Every last witch sent to the gallows.
Chorus	The dream and the nightmare From which he can't wake.

Betty Parris and Abigail Williams run forward.

Betty Parris	She pinches my flesh!
Abigail Williams	She pricks me with pins!
Chorus	Their dream too The afflicted girls Daughters of Salem, its wounded children.

Ann Putnam, Mercy Lewis, and Mary Walcott run forward.

Ann Putnam	She bites, she tears!
Mercy Lewis	She twists my limbs!
Mary Walcott	She squeezes my heart!
Chorus	A fevered dream That holds them in torment

13

The grip of nightmare
That will not let them go.

The five girls cry out at the same time.

Betty Parris	She pinches my flesh!
Abigail Williams	She pricks me with pins!
Ann Putnam	She bites, she tears!
Mercy Lewis	She twists my limbs!
Mary Walcott	She squeezes my heart!

*As they cry out, **the magistrates** speak over them.*

Nicholas Noyes   See how the witch afflicts these poor children!

John Hathorne   We find her guilty, and she will hang!

The girls fall silent.

Chorus   And these, the magistrates,
It holds them too
Gripped in a nightmare of judgement and sentence
Like a noose that tightens around their throats.

*The magistrates speak to **Sarah Good**.*

Nicholas Noyes   Confess, witch, to your damnable crimes!

John Hathorne   Confess, and even now you shall be saved!

Sarah Good cries out.

Sarah Good   You're liars! I'm no witch! And if you take my life, you'll drink black blood!

Chorus   She flings her curse over our heads
And it hangs above us
It spreads its black wings
And this is the nightmare that holds us fast
All of us trapped in this same bad dream
The dark labyrinth of guilt and terror
And there's no way out
There's no escape
From the dream of the noose

The dream of the gallows
The dream of the woman falling through air
Our dream, our nightmare
That holds us fast
And keeps us here
And it won't let us wake.

The magistrates cry out.

Nicholas Noyes   Hang her!

John Hathorne   Hang the witch!

The whole Chorus take up the chant again.

Chorus   Hang her, hang the witch! Hang her, hang the witch! Hang her, hang the witch! Hang her, hang the witch! . . . *etc.*

As the voices grow louder, Mary Warren rises to her feet and cries out.

Mary Warren   No – no – I will tell – I will speak – hear me speak – !

But the Chorus do not listen to her. The Hangman places the noose around Sarah Good's neck and steps aside.

Chorus   Hang her! Hang the witch! Hang her! Hang the witch! Hang her! Hang the witch! . . . *etc.*

As the voices rise to a climax, Mary cries out once more.

Mary Warren   We did but dissemble!

Her cry silences the voices. There is silence. Lights go to sudden blackout.

ACT 1: SAINTS OF LIGHT

• •

SCENE 1

Salem Village centre.

*Lights rise slowly. The Chorus are standing as before, staring up at the gallows. But Sarah Good is no longer there. The gallows are empty. The **Chorus** turn and speak individually to the audience. As they do, **each Chorus member** crosses the stage to take up a position, seated or standing at the side of the stage. They remain here throughout the entire play, coming forward to speak when required, as chorus member, or character.*

Chorus   Salem Village in the state of Massachusetts
A few miles inland from the port of Salem Town
A community of farmers
Craftsmen and tradesmen
We live simply
We live sparingly
Hard-working
God-fearing
Disciplined and dutiful
Our days devoted to toil and prayer
A fellowship bound with brotherly affection
One fellowship under the law of God.

*During the following, **Parris** comes forward accompanied by his wife **Elizabeth**, their daughter **Betty**, their niece **Abigail Williams**, and their slave **Tituba**, who looks after the girls. They have just arrived, and **two or three carriers** follow with their belongings in cases. **The carriers** set the cases down centre stage, and **Parris** and his **family** stand among them.*

And this is Samuel Parris
Arrived here from Boston
With his wife and his daughter

His niece and his slave
In the fall of the year 1689
Samuel Parris, man of God,
Soon to be Minister of Salem Village.

• •

SCENE 2

*Parris speaks to **the carriers**.*

Samuel Parris   Set them down here and wait. I'll need you to take them into the house.

The carriers set the cases down and stand to one side.

Elizabeth Parris   May we not go inside now, Samuel?

Samuel Parris   We have to wait for the key.

Elizabeth Parris   I'm feeling rather tired – a little weak –

Samuel Parris   Sit on one of the cases. Betty, see to your mother. *[Betty helps Elizabeth to sit]*

*Jonathan Walcott approaches **Parris**.*

Jonathan Walcott   Samuel Parris?

Samuel Parris   Yes.

Jonathan Walcott	Jonathan Walcott. Thomas Putnam is my brother-in-law. He told me to look out for you.
Samuel Parris	Mr Walcott, yes. Mr Putnam has mentioned your name –
Betty Parris	Father –
Samuel Parris	*[Angrily]* You interrupt me, child, while I am speaking!
Betty Parris	Excuse me, Father –
Samuel Parris	There is no excuse!
Abigail Williams	But Uncle –
Samuel Parris	You as well, Abigail! Do you both mean to cross me – ?
Tituba	Master – Mistress isn't well.
Samuel Parris	What? Elizabeth – ?
Elizabeth Parris	I'm sorry, Samuel –
Tituba	I think she will faint –
Samuel Parris	I see. Mr Walcott, it has been a long journey and my wife is tired –
Jonathan Walcott	My uncle keeps the tavern close by. She can rest there.
Samuel Parris	Thank you. Betty, Abigail, go with her. And you, Tituba. Let your mistress take only water. It will be enough to revive her. I shall wait here for Mr Putnam.
Tituba	Yes, master.
	*Walcott leads them off. **Betty** and **Abigail** help **Elizabeth**. **Tituba** follows them. As this is happening, the **Chorus** speak.*
Chorus	So who is he, our new Minister?
	Just who is this Samuel Parris?
	I heard he studied at Harvard – but failed his exams
	Then he tried his hand at business – but it didn't work out
	Then he went to Barbados to run a plantation
	His father left it to him – but the enterprise collapsed
	So he came back to Boston and became a Minister –

And now he's here to be our Minister
And let's hope this time the job works out.

*Parris speaks to the **Chorus** and the audience.*

Samuel Parris   It's true, up till now my ventures have not been successful.
When I first came here from England I was full of hope and
plans. But there have been difficulties – unforeseen – setbacks,
reversals of fortune – though none of them have been of my
own making. Call it circumstance. The storms of life by which
I have been cruelly used. But I have weathered those storms.
God has guided me through them, His hand has sheltered me,
and led me here. For I believe it is by God's will that I am
come. That He means great work for me. And in Salem I shall
begin that work, and I shall carry it out with zeal and fervour.
To uphold the righteous. To seek out and fearfully chastise the
sinful. To proclaim anew God's kingdom. To fulfil my
destiny.

***Thomas Putnam** crosses to **Parris**.*

Thomas Putnam   Mr Parris. Thomas Putnam.

Samuel Parris   Mr Putnam, sir.

They shake hands.

Thomas Putnam   Welcome to Salem, Mr Parris. Welcome to your new ministry.

Samuel Parris   Indeed, Mr Putnam – if I do decide to take it up.

Thomas Putnam   There's some doubt?

Samuel Parris   You seemed to say so in your last letter. Regarding the
stipulations of my service here – there has been some
opposition –

Thomas Putnam   A few grumbling voices. They're nothing to be taken note of.
Be assured, sir, all your requirements will be met.

Samuel Parris   I'm glad of it – though I don't like to hear of these 'grumbling'
voices. Dissent does not go well in a community.

Thomas Putnam   I admit there is a faction here –

Samuel Parris	A faction – ?
Thomas Putnam	They are no great power –
Samuel Parris	I pray not, Mr Putnam. These are perilous times that we are living in. Satan is abroad in our colony. We must be ever watchful for his presence among us.
Thomas Putnam	And with your help we shall, Mr Parris. *[takes out a set of keys]* Here are the keys to the Minister's house. You will take them?
Samuel Parris	I will, Mr Putnam. *[takes the keys]* Call your committee together at the meeting house tomorrow morning, so that we can finalize the arrangements for my tenure. Good afternoon, Mr Putnam.
Thomas Putnam	Good afternoon to you, Mr Parris. And once again, welcome to Salem Village.

Parris turns to the carriers.

Samuel Parris	Bring those.

Parris goes. The carriers pick up the cases and take them off.

Putnam speaks to the audience.

Thomas Putnam	This Minister drives a hard bargain. What he's asked for doesn't sit well with some. But Salem Village must have its own church, and its own Minister ordained. That will give us right to council, to look after our own affairs. Then those of us of rank will have a voice that's heard, and we'll be a real power in this place at last. That's the mark I aim at, and I'll not be thwarted. Let those who oppose me growl and snarl. I have their names, and I'll have them silenced. And if they won't be, or if they snarl too fierce, the wrath of church and state will fall upon them – and it'll be their own graves they'll be digging.

Putnam goes.

SCENE 3

Near the meeting house, the next day.

***Francis Nurse, Isaac Easty, and Joseph Putnam** come forward.*

Isaac Easty	I was told he demands £60.
Joseph Putnam	Demands it, does he? Demands, not requests!
Francis Nurse	It's a steep sum.
Isaac Easty	It is, for a man newly-come to ministry.
Joseph Putnam	And as a last resort after all else has failed.
Francis Nurse	Let's not be uncharitable. He may have the call.
Isaac Easty	He calls upon us, sure enough. To grant him a salary of sixty pounds a year.

***Peter Cloyce** comes forward.*

Peter Cloyce	And corn at cost price. And firewood supplied to him free of charge. And the Minister's house made over to him in ownership.
Isaac Easty	He can't have that. The house is property of the village.
Joseph Putnam	He makes mighty high demands, this Minister. And thinks mighty high of himself too.
Isaac Easty	We must speak against this, friends.
Peter Cloyce	Speak against it all you like. It'll do no good.
Joseph Putnam	What do you mean?
Peter Cloyce	It's all been passed by committee. And every demand granted.
Francis Nurse	They've had their meeting already?
Peter Cloyce	This morning, early. I've just come from there.
Joseph Putnam	Why weren't we told of it?
Peter Cloyce	I suppose they reckoned there was no need, as the meeting

house was filled with the Putnam clan. Except for you, of course, Joseph.

Francis Nurse   This is your brother's doing.

Joseph Putnam   My half-brother. And you're right, Francis. It's his ambition brings this proud Minister among us. He'll have his church, now, and, if we're not watchful, with the church the town. But our voices still have weight. And we must make sure they're heard.

● ●

SCENE 4

The meeting house, Sunday.

Parris comes forward, to preach a sermon. As he does so, the Chorus speak.

Chorus   Now Salem has its Minister
Now Salem has its church
And on a cold Sunday in November
That church is gathered in the meeting house
Thomas Putnam and his family
Thomas Putnam and his friends
Gathered on a cold Sunday in November
To be warmed by the words of Samuel Parris.

Samuel Parris   Brethren. Men and women of Salem Village. Let us rejoice this day. Let us rejoice that God has brought us together in his church; that God has chosen us as His elect to do His will upon this earth. Let us give ourselves up unto the Lord, let us labour together and suffer together; let us be a comfort and a delight to each other; that the Lord be our God and dwell among us in the unity of the spirit and the bond of peace. Yes, let us rejoice. But let us also be wary. Let us be watchful for those that would bring division to this church. For there is good in the world and there is evil, and if a man will not serve the one he must serve the other. There may be saints in God's church but there are sinners also. And those who are saints know who they are, and those who are sinners know who they are; and though they may dissemble, Christ sees into their hearts, and the time shall come when they shall be known to all. Then their prayers shall turn to curses thrown upon their own heads, and they shall be cast out of the good land into the place of eternal torment, where they would give all for a single drop of water to quench the fires of their suffering. Look into your own hearts, brethren, and if Satan has found a place there, turn him out, and with your whole being embrace this church, so that all of us, as one community, one brotherhood, one fellowship without division, may be received into the inheritance of the Saints of Light. Amen.

• •

SCENE 5

Outside the meeting house.

Parris *turns to cross the stage. As he does so,* **Dorcas Good** *runs across and bumps into him. During their encounter, other characters gather from the* **Chorus** *to watch –* **Thomas Putnam** *and* **Jonathan Walcott** *together, and* **Rebecca Nurse, Mary Easty,** *and* **Sarah Cloyce** *together.*

Samuel Parris	What's this? Running on a Sunday? Know you not this is the Lord's day, and not made for sport and merriment? *[pause]* Do you stare at me? Won't you answer? Do you know who I am, child?
Dorcas Good	You are a tall man in a black coat.
Samuel Parris	Brazen creature! What are you? Give me your name! *[he grips her shoulders]* I'll have your name!
Rebecca Nurse	Her name is Dorcas Good.
Thomas Putnam	Sarah Good's her mother. A beggar.
Jonathan Walcott	A Godless woman. I've heard her curse when I've turned her from my tavern.
Thomas Putnam	And the child follows her mother's example.
Samuel Parris	*[To Dorcas]* Are you begging, child? And on the Lord's day?

23

God does not love beggars. You would do better to go home and say prayers for your salvation.

Jonathan Walcott I doubt she knows how to say one. The child and mother both are little better than heathens.

Mary Easty Don't be too hard with her. The poor child knows no better.

Sarah Cloyce She doesn't have the benefit of a Minister for a father to instruct her in the ways of righteousness.

Rebecca Nurse Dorcas, come to me. Here's an apple for you. *[She holds out an apple. **Dorcas** runs to her and takes it.]* Now go home to your mother. And walk. Remember it is the Sabbath.

Dorcas goes.

Thomas Putnam I wonder you should encourage the child in her slothful and sinful ways, Rebecca Nurse.

Rebecca Nurse Charity is best given to those most in need of it, Mr Putnam.

Jonathan Walcott	That child needs chastisement more than charity.
Mary Easty	It's prayer she needs, Mr Walcott. And if she can't pray for herself we must pray for her. As we must pray for all good Christian souls in need.
Samuel Parris	*[To Rebecca]* You are Goodwife Nurse?
Rebecca Nurse	I am, Mr Parris, and these are my sisters, Mary Easty and Sarah Cloyce.
Samuel Parris	Those names are known to me.
Thomas Putnam	They should be, Mr Parris. Their husbands were among those who opposed your ordination.
Sarah Cloyce	It was not your ordination they opposed, Mr Parris. But they did have some argument with its terms.
Mary Easty	But the matter is settled now, and they're content.
Jonathan Walcott	Not content enough to be at the gathering this morning.
Rebecca Nurse	That was nothing to do with the dispute. Francis had to travel to Salem Town on business yesterday and hasn't yet returned. I'm sure he attended the gathering there.
Sarah Cloyce	As for Peter, he's not well.
Mary Easty	And Isaac is visiting his brother in Andover.
Samuel Parris	Well, they have their reasons. But I hope to see them here next Sunday. We are one community in the Lord, and must be seen to be so, without division or faction.
Sarah Cloyce	If you look for division or discontent, Mr Parris, you'll not find it in our households.
Mary Easty	There's more than one faction in this village –
Rebecca Nurse	No more of that, Mary –
	*Tituba crosses to **Parris**, agitated.*
Tituba	Mr Parris, will you come home?
Samuel Parris	What is it, Tituba?

Tituba	Mistress Parris is asking for you –
Samuel Parris	Tell her I'll be there presently –
Tituba	I think you must come now, master –
Samuel Parris	Must – ?
Tituba	It's her affliction. She calls for you –
Samuel Parris	Very well, I'm coming.
Rebecca Nurse	Your wife's afflicted, Mr Parris. Is there anything I can do?
Sarah Cloyce	Rebecca's known for her healing –
Samuel Parris	She is – a little unwell, that's all – I can manage – please excuse me – good morning to you all –

Parris and Tituba go. The rest disperse back into the Chorus, except for Putnam and Walcott, who remain centre stage.

Jonathan Walcott	Did you mark that, Thomas? Goodwife Nurse was quick enough to offer her help to Mistress Parris.
Thomas Putnam	And Mr Parris was wise to turn it down. I think there's more harm than help in her supposed healing.
Jonathan Walcott	So I've heard say. Didn't your own wife suffer at her hands?
Thomas Putnam	She swears it was through her we lost the last child.
Jonathan Walcott	We must warn our Minister against her.
Thomas Putnam	He'll not need much warning. He's a sharp man. And ambitious. He knows who his friends are in this village.
Jonathan Walcott	And those who aren't. There are sinners as well as saints in God's church. And they know who they are.
Thomas Putnam	And so do we. And the time shall come when they shall be known to all.

They go.

SCENE *6*

*Elizabeth Parris enters as the **Chorus** speak.*

Chorus The Minister's wife is afflicted
That's what the Indian slave woman said
She stays in her home
She keeps to her bed
She stays in her room
She never goes out
The Minister's wife is afflicted.

Elizabeth Parris I was never strong. From a child I've been afflicted by chills,
fevers. In Barbados I almost died. When we came to Salem I
hoped things would improve. It was to be a new beginning, for
both of us. I looked forward to taking on my new role, and felt
certain that here I would at last grow strong.

Chorus The Minister's wife is afflicted
I've heard her weeping as I've passed by the house
Weeping, as if her body was shaking
Sobbing, as if her heart was breaking
And sometimes laughing
A strange, wild laughing that chills the blood
The Minister's wife is afflicted.

Elizabeth Parris But I didn't. My fevers returned. They grew worse. As if
something in Salem was afflicting me with dreams and visions.
And I can't tell my husband. A Minister's wife who has
visions? I daren't tell my husband. So I keep silent. And the
dreams continue.

Chorus The Minister's wife is afflicted
A strange affliction that troubles her soul
And they say that sometimes she walks in her sleep
She leaves her bed
She leaves her home
I passed her once, I was coming home late
I saw her walking the paths at night
But she didn't see me, though her eyes were open

And what did she see with her troubled eyes?
The Minister's wife is afflicted.

● ●

SCENE 7

Salem Village, night. **Elizabeth** *speaks in a waking dream.*

Elizabeth Parris What place is this? Where do I walk? In the valley of the shadow. Am I awake or dreaming? What's that? It is my husband praying. Have mercy on her soul. And there! Shadows, figures of men. Voices whispering, plotting. Why should the Minister have a house? To keep his wife in. His poor wife's afflicted. What ails her? Voices. Shadows. Yet I will fear no evil. Who whispers against me? Who accuses? I am the Minister's wife! You shall not accuse me! No! No more! Your voices hurt my ears! I will not listen!

Abigail Hobbs *has entered. She speaks to* **Elizabeth.**

Abigail Hobbs I hear them too.

Elizabeth Parris Who's there?

Abigail Hobbs Voices. Whispering. In the grass. In the leaves.

Elizabeth Parris What are you?

Abigail Hobbs And singing too. And dancing.

Elizabeth Parris Are you a spirit?

Abigail Hobbs There are spirits haunt the woods. I've seen them. There are women and children. And a tall man in a black coat. He leads them in their dancing. Sometimes I dance with them.

Elizabeth Parris Dancing is forbidden. It is a grievous sin.

Abigail Hobbs He takes hold of my arms and swings me round. Round and round. It's like I am flying.

Elizabeth Parris Do you fly?

Abigail Hobbs Others do. I could tell you their names. I think I've seen you there.

Elizabeth Parris	No – you haven't –
Abigail Hobbs	Once he laid me down in the grass and pressed himself to me.
Elizabeth Parris	I should not be here – this is no dream –
	Abigail Hobbs grasps Elizabeth's hand.
Abigail Hobbs	Come with me! Come to the woods! They are there! Let's join them!
Elizabeth Parris	No – leave me – !
Abigail Hobbs	Come! We'll sing and dance and fly!
Elizabeth Parris	Devil – let go – !
	Tituba and Samuel Parris enter.
Tituba	Master, she's here!
Samuel Parris	Elizabeth!
Abigail Hobbs	Come now – !
Samuel Parris	Take your hands off her!
	Parris drags Abigail Hobbs away from Elizabeth and throws Abigail to the floor.
Elizabeth Parris	Tituba!
Tituba	It's all right, mistress.
	She comforts Elizabeth.
Samuel Parris	*[To Abigail Hobbs]* Who are you?
Abigail Hobbs	Will you beat me, sir?
Samuel Parris	Tell me your name!
Abigail Hobbs	All know me. I am Abigail Hobbs.
Samuel Parris	And where are you from, Abigail Hobbs?
Abigail Hobbs	I live in Topsfield. It is close by Salem.
Samuel Parris	What are you doing out here at night?

Abigail Hobbs	Nothing, sir – I sometimes walk out of nights –
Samuel Parris	For what purpose?
Abigail Hobbs	For the liking of it.
Samuel Parris	You could be whipped for this!
Abigail Hobbs	I was doing no harm.
Samuel Parris	Only the wicked walk abroad at night!
Abigail Hobbs	Does that include your wife, sir?
Samuel Parris	What?
Abigail Hobbs	She said she was the Minister's wife and I know you are the minister –
Samuel Parris	How dare you – !
Abigail Hobbs	But I'm sure such as she could not be wicked – no more than an innocent child such as I –
Samuel Parris	An innocent child indeed. Who are your parents?
Abigail Hobbs	William and Deliverance Hobbs, sir.
Samuel Parris	Do they know you walk out at nights?
Abigail Hobbs	If they know they don't care. And I don't care if they know.
Samuel Parris	Go home to them. And say nothing of this. Say nothing of meeting my wife. Neither to them nor to anyone. Or I shall have you whipped, and you and your parents cast out of your homes.
Abigail Hobbs	It won't be the first time. We have been cast out before.

Samuel Parris turns to Elizabeth.

Samuel Parris	Elizabeth.
Elizabeth Parris	I do not know how I came here, Samuel. I was dreaming, and I woke and I was here – and the creature –
Samuel Parris	Think no more of her. Come. I'll take you home now. And we shall pray this affliction be lifted from you.

Parris takes Elizabeth off. Abigail Hobbs rises and speaks to Tituba.

Abigail Hobbs I danced with a man in the woods. A tall man in a black coat. I think he was a Minister.

She laughs and runs off. Tituba speaks to the audience.

Tituba They call my people savages, say we worship the Devil, and are devils ourselves. They say our hearts are wild and filled with darkness. But there are dark hearts beating in these folk too, and a fear and a wildness in their eyes. I've seen how they treat others of their kind, with beatings and with whippings and with hangings. In their church they pray to their God for peace, and make war among themselves. To my mind it's a savage God they worship. But I'm a slave and must be silent, until my masters bid me speak.

Tituba goes.

● ●

SCENE 8

The meeting house, some time later. Jonathan Walcott and Thomas Putnam enter.

Jonathan Walcott Who called this meeting, Thomas?

Thomas Putnam It was Mr Parris.

Jonathan Walcott What's the reason?

Thomas Putnam I don't know. He sent word to me only that it was urgent.

Jonathan Walcott It is very sudden. What others are attending?

Thomas Putnam I can't say. I had no time to inform any others.

Joseph Putnam enters, with Francis Nurse.

Joseph Putnam Then we'll make up the numbers.

Thomas Putnam Joseph. What brings you here? And you Francis Nurse?

Francis Nurse Any may attend who are friends to this village.

Jonathan Walcott	You're no friends to the village.
Joseph Putnam	What? Are you and your company the only friends the village has?
Francis Nurse	I think that's how they'd have it, Joseph.
Joseph Putnam	If that's so, then God have mercy on us.
	***Samuel Parris** enters.*
Samuel Parris	Who are you to speak of God and not set foot inside his church? And to make opposition to its appointed Minister?
Joseph Putnam	Your appointment wasn't agreed by us.
Francis Nurse	Nor was it ratified. And is still therefore a matter of debate.
Samuel Parris	And this is no doubt what you debated at your meeting yesterday.
Joseph Putnam	It was among the matters we considered.
Jonathan Walcott	Meeting? What meeting?
Thomas Putnam	We weren't told of any meeting.
Francis Nurse	There was no need. There were enough of us present.
Samuel Parris	Enough of you to put your names to this letter. *[he holds up the letter he has in his hand]* Here it is. Delivered to me last night by Francis Nurse. And it is nothing more nor less than an attack upon myself, and upon the church of Salem Village.

Joseph Putnam	You're too severe with us, Mr Parris. It is no attack upon you. But it does call into question the terms of your appointment.
Thomas Putnam	Let's see this letter.
Samuel Parris	By all means, Mr Putnam. Read it aloud, if you will.
Thomas Putnam	*[Reads]* 'At a general meeting of the Committee of Salem Village on October 16 – '
Jonathan Walcott	You're a committee, are you?
Francis Nurse	Yes, and duly appointed.
Thomas Putnam	By themselves, no doubt.
Samuel Parris	Read on, Mr Putnam.
Thomas Putnam	*[Reads]* ' – it was voted whether instruction should be given for the making of a rate for Mr Parris's salary for the coming year; it was voted in the negative.'
Samuel Parris	There! They refuse my salary!
Jonathan Walcott	They can't do that.
Samuel Parris	They would try. And more.
Thomas Putnam	*[Reads]* 'It was also voted to consider the matter of the village rights to the ministry house and land, which has been impaired and made void when given without sanction to Mr Parris; and to further consider the matter of the gift of firewood – '
Samuel Parris	You see? They would take all from me – my salary, my house, even my firewood! They would drive me from Salem.
Thomas Putnam	And take our church from us.
Joseph Putnam	Your church, is it, Thomas? The church of Putnam and his kin.
Francis Nurse	We mean to take nothing from you, Mr Parris. Our only wish is to negotiate new terms.
Jonathan Walcott	The terms aren't for negotiation. They were settled and agreed –
Joseph Putnam	Show us the paper where these agreements are written, and we'll consent to them.

Thomas Putnam	They don't need your consent.
Jonathan Walcott	It was a mistake not to write them down.
Thomas Putnam	Let's do it now, then. I have paper here. We'll set down the terms and sign our names –
Francis Nurse	No. They must be voted on.
Jonathan Walcott	There are too few of us for a vote –

Peter Cloyce and Isaac Easty enter.

Isaac Easty	There are enough of us now.
Peter Cloyce	We have a voice in this meeting.
Isaac Easty	And a vote.
Joseph Putnam	And this time whatever's agreed upon shall be written down, so there'll be no future misunderstanding of it.
Samuel Parris	You men – your names are also on this letter. This is a conspiracy against me!
Thomas Putnam	It isn't you they conspire against, Mr Parris. There's division between us goes back a long way. These men and their families have been no friends to me these many years.
Peter Cloyce	It's true, there's been dispute over land.
Isaac Easty	But this has nothing to do with it.
Peter Cloyce	It's a different matter entirely.
Joseph Putnam	And I never had quarrel with you, Thomas, until you forced this Minister and church upon us.
Jonathan Walcott	Forced the church! He speaks as if it were some evil thing.
Thomas Putnam	Perhaps for their kind it is.
Francis Nurse	Our kind? What do you call our kind?
Thomas Putnam	There's a name for them.
Peter Cloyce	Out with it, then.

Isaac Easty	Let's hear it.
Thomas Putnam	They that are enemies of the church.
Jonathan Walcott	They that are enemies of God.
Francis Nurse	We are no enemies of God, Jonathan Walcott. You know this. We are all good Christian men, and know our duty and our Bible.
Peter Cloyce	But we will have our say.
Isaac Easty	And we will have our vote.
Samuel Parris	No! There'll be no vote!
Joseph Putnam	With respect, Mr Parris, you have no say in this –
Samuel Parris	And you, sir, with respect, be mindful of who I am! Your minister! And I say that before there's any vote we must have prayer. We have grown too hot and testy in our words. Space and time are needed to cool them. And to look deep into our own hearts, and take care all that we find there's honest, and of good intent. Let's to our homes and pray, gentlemen. Then we shall meet again and in the grace of God settle this matter. But in the meantime, I'd have you take care of one thing more.
Joseph Putnam	And what might that be, Mr Parris?
Samuel Parris	I am without firewood.
	Parris goes.
Isaac Easty	It's a pity that our Minister has no firewood.
Peter Cloyce	It is, and with the weather turning cold.
Francis Nurse	We can't see him go without.
Isaac Easty	I'm a man of charity. I'll lend him my axe so that he may chop some.
	Laughing, they go.
Jonathan Walcott	See how they jest! They'll learn this is no laughing matter – !

Thomas Putnam	No more of that, Jonathan. We'll do as Mr Parris advises. To our homes and pray.

Jonathan Walcott goes.

Joseph Putnam	The business will be settled, Thomas.
Thomas Putnam	So it will. One way or another.

Joseph and Thomas go, separately.

• •

SCENE 9

Parris's house, a short time later. Parris enters.

Samuel Parris	I know their minds and their intent. They make it plain enough. They'd turn me out. That's their purpose. To cast out Minister and church from Salem Village. Thomas Putnam warned me against them. Men driven by envy, greed, ambition. Enemies of this village and its church. Enemies of Christ. And here among us, in our midst! God have mercy on us! *[calls out]* Tituba! Are you there? Tituba!

Tituba enters.

Tituba	Master?
Samuel Parris	Bring the children to me.
Tituba	Yes, master –
Samuel Parris	And Mrs Parris too.
Tituba	Mrs Parris – she's in her bed, master –
Samuel Parris	Then bring her from her bed. It's too late to be sleeping.
Tituba	She has her sickness –
Samuel Parris	We all have a sickness and there's only one cure for it. Bring her here!
Tituba	Yes, master.

Tituba goes.

Samuel Parris	Prayer. Prayer is the cure. Prayer is the weapon the Lord has placed in my hands. I alone am here to root out these devils and send them howling to perdition's fire. This is the purpose of my ministry. For this I was sent for. For this I was come.

Tituba enters with Betty, Abigail, and Elizabeth.

Children. Wife. Kneel with me. And you, Tituba. Let us kneel together and pray.

All kneel. Parris prays aloud.

O, Lord, there are devils in Christ's church, Satan's brood dwelling here among us. They would tear down thy holy city, O, Lord, throw open its shining gates and let in hell. Thou knowest them, Lord, their faces to thee are not hidden. And with thy grace we shall know them also, and cry out upon them. Be they neighbour or friend, sister or brother, they are an abomination to the people of the Lord, and shall be cast out. O, Lord, lend us thy strength for this great task, that we may cleanse this village of infection, and crush our enemies, and let fall thy wrath upon their heads!

Elizabeth, Betty, Abigail, and Tituba have been caught up in the prayer and begin to chant the last line with Parris, their voices growing louder, almost to the point of hysteria.

All   And let fall thy wrath upon their heads!
And let fall thy wrath upon their heads!
Let fall thy wrath!
Let fall thy wrath!
Let fall thy wrath!
Let fall thy wrath!

End of Act 1

ACT 2: YELLOW SNAKE

SCENE 1

*Salem Village, outside Parris's house. **Dorcas Good** enters,
running, with a crust of bread. She goes to centre stage, sits, and
tears hungrily at the bread. As she does this, **Betty Parris** and
Ann Putnam enter. They see **Dorcas** and sneak up on her.*

Ann Putnam	Where did you get that bread?
	Dorcas starts and turns.
Betty Parris	Answer the question, Dorcas Good.
Ann Putnam	How did you come by that bread?
Betty Parris	Did you steal it?
Ann Putnam	You must have stolen it.
Betty Parris	Who did you steal it from?
Ann Putnam	Tell us!
Dorcas Good	I didn't steal it.
Betty Parris	That's a lie.
Ann Putnam	Lying's a sin. A worse sin than stealing. The devil is the king of lies.
Betty Parris	You'll burn in hell for that lie, Dorcas Good.
Dorcas Good	It isn't a lie. I was give it.
Ann Putnam	*[Laughing]* She was give it.
Betty Parris	Who gave it to you?
Dorcas Good	Goody Nurse give it me.
Ann Putnam	You were begging off Goody Nurse.
Betty Parris	She begs off everybody. And her mother too.

Ann Putnam	Beggars should be whipped, that's what my father says.
Betty Parris	They are not honest folk. Honest folk work for their living. Those who beg are slothful, and they are Godless parasites.
Ann Putnam	You shall be whipped, Dorcas Good, you and your mother both.
Dorcas Good	No one shall whip me.
Ann Putnam	I'm Ann Putnam, and if I tell my father to have you whipped, you shall be whipped.
Dorcas Good	If you have me whipped I'll send my snake to bite you.
Betty Parris	What snake?
Dorcas Good	I have a pet snake.
Ann Putnam	You have no snake.
	*Dorcas stands. As she speaks, **Betty** and **Ann** become frightened, though they try not to show it.*
Dorcas Good	I do! He's yellow like gold and he comes when I call him. Sliding and hissing through the grass. Like this: hsssssssss! I feed him with my little finger. He sucks the blood out of it. But to others his bite is poisonous. And I will send him to bite you – and you – and you will fall into a fit and a fever and your limbs will swell and your skin will turn black and you will have cramps and pains and you shall die!
	*Betty and **Ann** stare at **Dorcas** for a moment, terrified. Then they recover themselves.*
Ann Putnam	You have no such power.
Betty Parris	And if you do, it is the power of Satan.
Ann Putnam	The snake is the Devil's creature.
Betty Parris	I shall tell my father and he will proclaim you from the pulpit for a child of Satan!
Ann Putnam	And you will be cast out of the village! And your mother with you!

Dorcas Good	*[Suddenly nervous]* There is no snake – it was idle talk –
Ann Putnam	Then you may tramp the roads and go beg from the natives.

Sarah Good has entered, unseen by the children. She comes forward now.

Sarah Good	Who talks of casting me out the village? Is it you, Ann Putnam, and you, Betty Parris? And is it you putting fear into my poor child? *[to Dorcas]* Come here to me, Dorcas. *[Dorcas runs to her. She speaks again to Betty and Ann.]* You say nothing and show me innocent faces, but I know what hides beneath them. I see the scorn in your eyes. Who are you to scorn those less favoured by fortune? Mighty high the two of you think you are, no doubt. And mighty high and fine you may well be. As I was once, till fortune brought me low. And what I say to you is, take care of fortune, that it does not bring you down one day as low as I am now. And if it should, I pray I'm there to see it.

Tituba enters.

Tituba	Betty. Your father calls for you. And for you, Miss Putnam. You're both to go into the house.

Relieved at being saved, Betty and Ann back away from Sarah Good, then turn and go. Tituba speaks to Sarah.

I have word for you from Mr Parris.

Sarah Good	Have you, now? I suppose I'd better hear it.
Tituba	Mr Parris says that if you persist in your begging ways you are to keep clear of his home and of the church.
Sarah Good	He does, does he?
Tituba	And keep your daughter clear as well. And most especially she is not to have association with his daughter, and those under his care.
Sarah Good	This is a fine thing, to be given command by a slave.
Tituba	I may be a slave, but I am slave to Mr Parris. I work for my keep and am no beggar woman.

Sarah Good	*[Savagely]* And I am free-born and a Christian and no native heathen that worships devils and drinks the blood of white men! *[she speaks to **Dorcas**]* Come, Dorcas. There's no charity in Salem Village while its minister keeps savages in his house.
Dorcas Good	*[To **Tituba**]* The yellow snake will come for you.
	*Sarah and Dorcas go. **Tituba** calls after them.*
Tituba	I am no heathen! I am Christian too! I was baptized! *[more softly, to herself]* I am Christian too.
	She goes.

• •

SCENE 2

	*Inside Parris's house, a short time later. **Parris** enters with **Betty** and **Ann**.*
Samuel Parris	I saw you from my window. Do you deny you spoke with her?
Betty Parris	No, Father. We do not deny it.
Samuel Parris	Against my express wishes! I had forbidden it!
Ann Putnam	It was she who spoke with us first, Mr Parris.
Samuel Parris	Do not make defence for yourself, Ann Putnam. Your father would not be pleased to find that you have defied me.
Ann Putnam	No, Mr Parris. He would not.
Samuel Parris	You have a position here in Salem. You are the children of men who have a standing among its inhabitants. And with that standing and that position comes a duty. To obey the will of God in all matters. And to you children your fathers' will is as the will of God. And it is beyond all questioning. Is that clear to you?
Betty Parris	Yes, Father.
Ann Putnam	Yes, Mr Parris.

*During the following, **Parris** forgets he is speaking to **the girls** and takes on the role of preacher, speaking to an imagined congregation. As he is doing this, **Tituba** enters and observes.*

Samuel Parris   Obedience is all. Our society stands by obedience. It falls by the lack of it. Was not disobedience the first sin? Was it not through disobedience that Adam fell and was cast out of Eden? It is a most grievous sin, this sin of disobedience, and it marks Man out for death. Death is our lot, it is the inheritance we have received from our first father, for his sin of disobedience. And death may strike us down at any time. Do you think that you are not marked out for death? Do you believe you are too young to die? Children! Go to the burying ground. There you will see many graves smaller than your own may be. They that lie in them were not too young to die. You are not too young to die. And when death comes, as come it will, are you prepared? Are your souls in readiness? Because if they are not you will be damned, and you will suffer for eternity the wretched pains and torments of hell!

*He turns back to **Betty** and **Ann**.*

On your knees, children. On your knees and pray that your souls may be pure and that you will no longer commit this sin of disobedience.

*In utter fear **Betty** and **Ann** fall to their knees, bow their heads, clasp their hands and pray. **Parris** turns to **Tituba**.*

Watch over them. See they do not stir till I return.

Parris goes.

SCENE 3

*Ann and **Betty** kneel with heads bowed and hands clasped.*
***Tituba** stands behind them. The **Chorus** speak. At the same time,*
Abigail Williams** enters from one side of the stage, and **Mercy
***Lewis** from the other.*

Chorus

We came here to find God's country
Crossed the sea to create the Lord's kingdom
Build His shining city
Here in this new world
But what we found was a land of fear
A wilderness of shadows and wicked spirits
Whose savage faces stared out from the trees
Whose bloody drums beat in the heathen dark.

Mercy Lewis

The first coming of the savages was at sunrise. Within a few minutes some of the farms were burning and the air was filled with gunshots and screams. I saw a boy running from one of the houses. He tripped and fell and the next moment the heathen were upon him and knocked him on the head with their hatchets. A woman came from another house holding a babe in arms. She raised one hand and cried for mercy but they fired upon her, killing her and the child both. Then my mother began to weep, for it appeared the Lord had abandoned us and we were all filled with fear.

Chorus

Fear and darkness
A nightmare country
Hills and forests haunted by demons
We hear their voices howling, yelping
The baying tongues of lost souls
Hell's creatures gathered to work their evil
To butcher our bodies and snatch our souls
And to fill our dreams
With darkness and fear.

*Betty and **Ann** pray aloud.*

Betty Parris   I will call upon the Lord and He shall save me.

Ann Putnam   I will cry aloud and He shall hear my voice.

Betty Parris   Deliver me from my enemies.

Ann Putnam   Save me from bloodthirsty men.

Abigail Williams   We were at the harbour and there was a great crowd gathered there. Most were women. There was news that our men had captured some savages in their canoes. Someone said to me that I would now see the faces of those that had killed my mother and father. At last a boat came into the harbour and the men came ashore leading five or six Indians with their hands bound. Everyone started to press forward, but someone lifted me up so that I could see the Indians. One of them looked straight at me. I saw his painted face and his dark eyes staring into mine. And there was murder in them and bloodshed, and I wanted to cry out but my tongue would not move, nor my whole body, and I was rigid with terror for my mortal soul, for I was gazing into the very face of my fear.

*The **Chorus** begin to close in on **Tituba**.*

Chorus   This is the face of the one we fear
                        The one not like us
                        The stranger, the shadow
                        The one cast out from God's holy grace
                        Who dwells in the darkness beyond our borders
                        Who speaks the language of curse and blasphemy
                        The doomed, the damned
                        The alien, the other
                        Whose bloody hand reaches into our hearts
                        And plants our souls with shadows and fear.

*Betty and **Ann** pray aloud.*

Betty Parris   But the wicked shall perish –

Ann Putnam   And the enemies of the Lord –

Betty Parris   Like the splendour of the meadows shall vanish –

Ann Putnam	Into smoke they shall vanish away.
Mercy Lewis	My father and brothers were fallen and covered in blood, the house was burning over our heads, and there was nothing for it but to unfasten the door and to try and make our escape.
Abigail Williams	The townsfolk asked what would be done with the savages, and the men who had them captive said they would be taken to Boston for trial, but the townsfolk cried out no, they must be punished for their crimes.
Mercy Lewis	But no sooner had we left than bullets flew thick all around us and one went through my arm –
Abigail Williams	Then there was a great noise of shouting as the townsfolk demanded vengeance for their loved ones killed by the infidels –
Mercy Lewis	– and my mother and my sister dropped to the ground, and the hell-hounds came forward yelping with their hatchets raised –
Abigail Williams	– and they pressed forward in a great mass and took hold of the Indians and dragged them from their captors –
Mercy Lewis	– stripping the clothes from the dead, finishing the wounded with blows to the head, and all the time howling and roaring –
Abigail Williams	– crying out with curses and oaths, as they struck at them with stones and wooden stakes –
Mercy Lewis	– and it was a great sorrow and terror to me to see so many Christians slain like sheep torn by wolves, and of all my family only I living.
Abigail Williams	– and being a child I was kept back as they fell upon them, and did not see what had been done until they had finished their business and the savages were killed.

*The **Chorus** close in around **Tituba** so that she cannot be seen.*

Chorus	But we will not live in fear and shadow God sent us to purge this land of evil To take possession of it To drive out the darkness

And when the last savage is tamed or dead
Then it will become God's country
And we'll bless this earth and call it ours
And live free of all wickedness
Cleansed and pure
And dwell no more in shadow
And darkness and fear.

Betty and Ann pray aloud.

Betty Parris   His descendants will be mighty on earth!

Ann Putnam   The generations of the upright will be blessed!

• •

SCENE 4

Parris's house, some time later. **Abigail** *and* **Mercy** *run forward to join* **Betty** *and* **Ann**. *All four girls sit together, each with a homemade doll.* **Betty** *holds up her doll.*

Betty Parris   This is Sarah Good. See how she waddles like an old fat sow.

They laugh. **Ann** *takes the doll from her.*

Ann Putnam   And hear how she whines. *[she speaks in mockery of* **Sarah Good***]* 'Take care of fortune, that it does not bring you down one day as low as I am now.'

Abigail takes the doll from **Ann**.

Abigail Williams   See how low she has fallen.

She holds the doll up high then brings it down hard on to the floor. All laugh again.

Mercy Lewis   Poor creature! She has broken every bone in her body.

Betty takes up another doll.

Betty Parris   This is Dorcas Good.

Abigail Williams   I know it is. She smells like a midden.

Ann Putnam	Make her stand back. The stink of her will kill her mother.
Betty Parris	*[Speaking in mockery of **Dorcas**]* Oh, Mother! Get up! What shall we do? Who will go begging for us now?
	Mercy takes up a third doll.
Mercy Lewis	Here comes Rebecca Nurse to heal her.
Betty Parris	*[Speaking as **Dorcas**]* Goodwife Nurse! My poor mother is sorely hurt!
Mercy Lewis	*[Speaking as **Rebecca**]* What ails her, child?
Betty Parris	*[Speaking as **Dorcas**]* She has broke all her bones and cannot beg no more.
Mercy Lewis	*[Speaking as **Rebecca**]* Sarah Good, how did you come to break your bones?
Ann Putnam	*[Speaking as **Sarah**]* Through flying.
Mercy Lewis	*[Speaking as **Rebecca**]* You were flying, were you?
Betty Parris	*[Speaking as **Dorcas**]* Yes, my mother can fly, and I can fly as well. Like this.
	***Betty** wheels her doll through the air.*
Mercy Lewis	*[Speaking as **Rebecca**]* Oh! 'Tis a wicked thing to fly.
Abigail Williams	I saw you flying, Mercy Lewis.
Mercy Lewis	Me? No, you did not!
Abigail Williams	I did. I was sleeping and I woke and looked out of the window and you were flying above the woods.
Betty Parris	Do you fly, Mercy?
Mercy Lewis	No. It was but a dream of Abigail's –
	***Abigail** holds up a doll and flies it through the air.*
Abigail Williams	Here is Mercy Lewis flying!
Mercy Lewis	It's only a doll. I do not fly!

Betty Parris	Don't take on so, Mercy. It's but a game.
Mercy Lewis	It's not a game I like.
Ann Putnam	Do not play, then. But we shall. *[she snatches the doll from Mercy, and speaks as **Rebecca** to Abigail's doll]* You wicked, wicked child! Who taught you to fly?
Abigail Williams	*[Speaking as **Mary**]* It was Sarah Good taught me.
Ann Putnam	*[Speaking as **Rebecca**]* Sarah Good!
Betty Parris	*[Speaking as **Dorcas**]* That's right. She taught us both.
Ann Putnam	*[Speaking as **Rebecca**]* Sarah Good! You taught these children to fly! It is a terrible sin and you must be punished for it!
Abigail Williams	Yes! She must be punished!
Betty Parris	How shall we punish her?
Abigail Williams	Give her a whipping!
Betty Parris	Tar and feather her!
Abigail Williams	Throw her in gaol!
Betty Parris	Throw her in the river!
Ann Putnam	*[Dropping the Rebecca Nurse doll]* No! These are all too mild! Let her be stuck with a pin!
	*Ann holds up a long sharp pin, and picks up the Sarah Good doll. **The other children** are shocked into momentary silence. Then Mercy speaks.*
Mercy Lewis	This is wrong! To stick a pin into a doll. It is like –
Ann Putnam	Who are you to say what is right or wrong, Mercy Lewis? You are only my father's servant! *[to the others]* There's no harm in it. Is there?
Abigail Williams	No. There's no harm.
Ann Putnam	Shall I do it, then?
Betty Parris	Yes. Yes! Go on!

Ann Putnam	Then let Sarah Good be punished for flying.
Betty Parris	And Dorcas Good for flying as well.
Abigail Williams	And Rebecca Nurse – for she has evil eyes.
	Ann raises the pin above the doll.
Ann Putnam	Sarah Good, prepare to meet thy doom!

*As **Ann** is about to bring the pin down, **Tituba** breaks through from the **Chorus**.*

Tituba	No!
	***The girls** start in surprise and fear. **Ann** quickly hides the pin.*
	Betty, Abigail! Those dolls – you know your father forbids such things in his house.
Abigail Williams	They're not ours.
Betty Parris	Ann Putnam and Mercy Lewis brought them.
Ann Putnam	It was Mercy made them. I did not.
Mercy Lewis	I meant no harm in it.
Tituba	What will your father say, Betty, when he knows of your passing time in such a way?

49

Betty Parris	You will not tell him?
Tituba	You'll have me keep secrets from him?
Betty Parris	We won't play with them again.
Tituba	I have my duty.
Abigail Williams	Don't tell my uncle, Tituba.
Tituba	If I choose to –
Ann Putnam	She has no choice. She is a slave. She must do as she is bid.
Tituba	I do Mr Parris's bidding, not yours, nor theirs. And with Mrs Parris ill I have been set to watch over them.
Betty Parris	You are a slave and you will do as you're bid.
Ann Putnam	You will do as we bid. You will not tell.

*The girls rise, and begin to advance on **Tituba**, encircling her. They chant, softly at first, their voices growing louder.*

Girls	You will not tell.
	You will not tell.
	You will not tell.
	You will not tell.
Abigail Williams	Or we'll put frogs and spiders in your bed.
Betty Parris	And snakes.
Ann Putnam	The yellow snake will come and bite you.
Mercy Lewis	And you'll have terrible dreams.
Abigail Williams	And ghosts will haunt you.
Betty Parris	And devils will torment you.
Ann Putnam	And the black horse will come and drag you away.
Mercy Lewis	Away through the air and you'll never come back.

*The girls hold hands and run round **Tituba** in a circle, crying out.*

Girls	Wheeeeeeeeeeee!

Tituba	Stop! *[they stop]* Very well. I won't tell. But take those things out of this house. Get rid of them. Burn them.
Ann Putnam	We can't do that, Tituba. We can't burn them. If we did, just think how they would scream.

The girls grab their dolls from the floor and run to one side of the stage, laughing. They sit there in a huddle. Tituba recovers herself, and speaks to the audience.

Tituba	This is a bad dream. But it is not my dream. It is theirs. These children's, the people of this village. Their own nightmare story. I have no story. I am a slave, a savage, the stranger in the shadows. I am a person without a story. Even my name is uncertain. But now they have made me a part of their story. I am walking into it out of the shadows. Now their story has become my story as well. And my acts shall be spoken of, and my voice shall be heard. And my name shall be written.

Tituba moves to one side of the stage, opposite the girls.

· ·

SCENE 5

The same, Parris's house. Ann holds a candle. The girls speak to each other confidentially.

Ann Putnam	Shall we look into the future?
Abigail Williams	What do you mean?
Ann Putnam	Let us see what the future holds for us.
Betty Parris	How shall we do that?
Ann Putnam	Mary Walcott showed me.

Mary Walcott enters. She carries a glass of water and an egg.

Mary Walcott	You have a glass of water and you have an egg. You break the egg into the water. Then you light a candle and hold its flame to the glass. And by the light of the flame you see the shape of your future, and it shall be known by all.

Betty Parris	Let's try it!
Abigail Williams	I want to see the future!

Mary Walcott approaches the girls.

Mary Walcott	What about your father?
Betty Parris	He's upstairs writing his sermon.
Mary Walcott	And your mother?
Abigail Williams	Aunt's ill. She won't disturb us.
Mercy Lewis	But is it right?
Ann Putnam	What do you mean?
Mercy Lewis	Looking into the future – it has to do with spell-making and magic.
Mary Walcott	Only in a small way.
Mercy Lewis	But is it not a sin?
Abigail Williams	It's only a sin if somebody knows.
Betty Parris	It's only a sin if somebody tells.
Mary Walcott	It's only a sin if we're found out.
Ann Putnam	And nobody's going to find out.

Parris enters centre stage and speaks an extract from his sermon.

Samuel Parris	There are devils in Christ's church. Christ knows how many of these devils there are. And Christ knows who these devils are.

*Elizabeth Parris enters on the opposite side of the stage to **the girls** and speaks to the audience out of the fever of her illness.*

Elizabeth Parris	I hear him. His voice low and soft. Outside the window. Come from the shadows to call me. He that the wild girl spoke of. He that dwells in the woods and leads them in the dancing. And I know it is no dream and I know he is there and he calls me to join in the dancing.

*On the other side of the stage **the girls** prepare their spell.*

Mary Walcott	First, light the candle.
	Betty lights the candle.
	Now take the glass.
	Ann takes the glass.
	Pour the water in the glass.
	Abigail pours the water.
	Break the egg into the water.
	Mercy breaks the egg.
	Hold up the candle.
	Betty holds up the candle.
	And let us see what will be shown.
	The girls gaze into the water. Centre stage, Parris speaks.
Samuel Parris	Thou knowest them, Lord, their faces to thee are not hidden. And with thy grace we shall know them also.
	Elizabeth Parris begins to grow more distracted.
Elizabeth Parris	Now he is here. He has come into my room. He stands by my bedside, a shadow above me. His face is in darkness. I cannot see it. Murmuring softly. Calling me away. Calling me to the dark and the dancing!
	On the other side of the stage, Betty stares into the glass by the light of the candle.
Abigail Williams	What do you see?
Betty Parris	I don't know.
Mercy Lewis	Is there anything there?
Betty Parris	I'm not sure.
Mary Walcott	There must be something.
Betty Parris	There is something –

Ann Putnam	What? What is it?
Betty Parris	I think – it's a face –
Ann Putnam	A face! Whose face? Whose face can you see? Tell us! Tell us!

*The girls chant softly, their voices growing louder as **Parris** speaks his prayer and **Elizabeth** speaks her dream above them.*

Girls	Tell us! Tell us! Tell us! Tell us! . . . etc.
Samuel Parris	They are an abomination!
Elizabeth Parris	He comes closer!
Samuel Parris	They shall be cast out.
Elizabeth Parris	Now I see his face!
Samuel Parris	And suffer the pains and torments of hell!
Elizabeth Parris	I know who it is!
Girls	Tell us! Tell us! Tell us!

Betty Parris cries out in terror.

Betty Parris	No! No! No! *[she screams]*

Parris turns to the children.

Samuel Parris	Children! What are you doing? What's the matter?

The girls do not look at him, but speak, as if in a trance.

Betty Parris	He grips my throat.
Girls	He grips my throat.
Betty Parris	He twists my limbs!
Girls	He twists my limbs!
Betty Parris	He burns my flesh!
Girls	He burns my flesh!
Samuel Parris	What do you mean? What is it? *[he shouts]* What is it? Tell me!

The girls turn to look at him, and huddle together in fear. They say nothing, but Elizabeth Parris speaks.

Elizabeth Parris   It is Death.

She turns and goes.

● ●

SCENE *6*

*The action is split between Parris's house and the village. **The girls** remain crouched on the floor in terror. The **Chorus** come forward.*

Chorus   The Minister's children are afflicted
His daughter, his niece
Afflicted by some strange malady
No one knows the cause
It happened suddenly
Cries were heard coming from the Minister's house
Shrieks and howls
Like the cries of wild animals
Or the demonic wailing of imps and spirits
But it wasn't wild animals
It wasn't imps or spirits
It was the Minister's children
Reverend Parris, minister of Salem
The Minister's children afflicted.

***Thomas Putnam** and **Jonathan Walcott** enter and speak to Parris.*

Thomas Putnam   What's the reason for this?

Jonathan Walcott   There must be some cause.

Thomas Putnam   It happened in your house, Parris!

Samuel Parris   You say I am the cause? When it is my own child who suffers!

Jonathan Walcott   They are our children who suffer as well.

Thomas Putnam   We are all touched by this.

Jonathan Walcott   And if any knows of a cause, none is better placed than you.

Samuel Parris	I know of no cause! How should I? I was not with them when it happened.
Thomas Putnam	Who was?
Samuel Parris	Only my slave.
Jonathan Walcott	The Indian woman.
Thomas Putnam	Have you questioned her?
Samuel Parris	Of course I have. I have questioned her severely. She can give no reason.
Jonathan Walcott	Or will not.
Thomas Putnam	A reason must be found. And then a cure. This must not continue long.
Jonathan Walcott	Word is spreading through the village, and beyond.
Thomas Putnam	We are becoming a story and a by-word.
	They go.
Chorus	I've been there
	I've seen them
	The poor, afflicted children
	It's terrifying, fascinating
	Horrible, but you have to look
	They writhe on the floor
	They crawl under chairs
	They twist their arms and legs into knots
	They bend their backs almost in two
	Poor children, to suffer such pains and torments
	And what's the reason?
	What's the cause?
	The doctors have tried but they can't discover it
	It must be something beyond natural healing
	A sickness of the soul
	An ailment of the spirit
	Children afflicted
	Children possessed.

Rebecca Nurse, Mary Easty, and Sarah Cloyce enter.

Rebecca Nurse   Possession has been spoken of.

Sarah Cloyce   Possession? Who speaks of it?

Rebecca Nurse   Doctor Griggs. He says there can be no other cause.

Mary Easty   It's beyond his skill so he places the blame on imps and spirits.

Sarah Cloyce   Yet there may be something in it.

Mary Easty   You think so, Sarah?

Sarah Cloyce   I believe there is something more than natural in what ails them.

Rebecca Nurse   Perhaps so. But the Devil? That's too strong.

Sarah Cloyce   It has been known before. There's written testimony.

Mary Easty   And it's widely read and known. There's more of devilment than the Devil in these girls' antics.

Rebecca Nurse   Yet neither do I think they counterfeit. What I saw of their suffering was most piteous.

Sarah Cloyce   Betty Parris does have a nervous nature, like her mother's.

Mary Easty   And Ann Putnam has a nature like her father's, a scheming and a devious one.

Rebecca Nurse   Mary, it is not well to speak so. Whatever the cause, we should have nothing but pity in our hearts for these poor children. And pray that the good Lord sees fit to release them from their affliction soon.

Rebecca goes.

Sarah Cloyce   Rebecca's right. We should pray.

Mary Easty   Indeed we should. For if the Devil's not abroad then mischief may be. And I fear the making of that more than of any witchcraft.

They go.

Chorus	There's witchery in Salem
	Sorcery and witchcraft in Salem Village
	The Devil's come to work his wickedness
	Wreak havoc among God's people
	We've heard of it happening in other villages
	And we always feared it would here
	And now it is, it is happening here
	Sorcery and witchcraft in Salem Village
	The Minister's children afflicted
	And the friends of the Minister's children
	And the friends of the Minister's children's friends
	All of them afflicted in the Minister's house
	Sorcery and witchcraft
	Sorcery and witchcraft
	Sorcery and witchcraft in Salem Village
	Sorcery and witchcraft in the Minister's house.

Parris, Putnam, and Walcott.

Samuel Parris	They must be questioned.
Jonathan Walcott	We must discover who it is that afflicts them.
Thomas Putnam	Before others question them and pass judgement.
Samuel Parris	We know what they're saying.
Jonathan Walcott	Where there's bewitchment there may also be witchery.
Thomas Putnam	They'd accuse our girls.
Samuel Parris	They'd accuse us.
Jonathan Walcott	Our foes and enemies are ranged against us.
Thomas Putnam	We must act first, before they act.
Samuel Parris	Question the girls.
Jonathan Walcott	Free their tongues.
Thomas Putnam	Make them accuse.

*They approach **the girls**, and stand around them. The **Chorus** chant.*

Chorus	Sorcery and witchcraft
	Sorcery and witchcraft
	Sorcery and witchcraft in Salem Village
	Sorcery and witchcraft
	Sorcery and witchcraft
	Sorcery and witchcraft in the Minister's house.

Parris, Walcott, and Parris question the girls.

Samuel Parris	Poor children.
Girls	Poor children.
Jonathan Walcott	You are afflicted.
Girls	Afflicted.
Thomas Putnam	You are bewitched.
Girls	Bewitched.
Samuel Parris	Someone means you harm.
Girls	Harm.
Jonathan Walcott	Someone causes you pain.
Girls	Pain.
Thomas Putnam	Someone puts your souls in torment.
Girls	Our souls in torment.
Samuel Parris	Who is it?
Girls	Who is it?
Jonathan Walcott	Tell us the name.
Girls	The name.
Thomas Putnam	Who is the witch?
Girls	The witch.

Parris pleads with the girls.

Samuel Parris	You must tell us. Give us the name. Who is it that bewitches you?

Whose spirit comes to you at night and torments you? There is one. There must be. Close your eyes. See the face of your tormentor. Now tell us the name. Speak it. For the good of your souls, for the safety of us all, tell us who it is! Tell us the name!

Tituba enters and speaks to Parris.

Tituba	Master –

The girls gasp in shock and turn to stare at Tituba.

Samuel Parris	What? Is this the one? Her? Is it Tituba?
Tituba	Master?

Betty cries out.

Betty Parris	Yes! It's Tituba! Tituba harms us. Tituba torments us. Tituba afflicts us. Tituba bewitches us. It's her! Tituba! Tituba's the witch!

Abigail, Ann, Mercy, and Mary point at Tituba.

Abigail Williams	The witch.
Ann Putnam	The witch.
Mercy Lewis	The witch.
Mary Walcott	The witch.

All the girls cry out together.

Girls	The witch!

Tituba cries out in fear.

Tituba	No!

*The **Chorus** turn their attention to **Tituba**, moving in to encircle her as they chant.*

Chorus   Now we see the face of our enemy
Now we know our enemy's name.

Tituba   I am no witch.

Chorus   The stranger
The alien
The heathen
The savage

Tituba   I practise no magic.

Chorus   The one who afflicts us
The one who torments us

Tituba   I call up no spirits.

Chorus   And fills our dreams with darkness and fear.

Tituba   I am no witch!

***Parris**, **Walcott**, and **Putnam** turn to **Tituba**.*

Samuel Parris   You deny it?

Tituba   Yes.

Jonathan Walcott   Why do they name you?

Tituba   I don't know.

Thomas Putnam   They say you torment them.

Tituba   I torment no one.

*The **girls** cry out.*

Betty Parris   She pinches my flesh!

Abigail Williams   She pricks me with pins!

Ann Putnam   She bites, she tears!

Mary Walcott   She grips my throat!

Mercy Lewis	She stops my breath!
Samuel Parris	Confess and you shall be saved.
Jonathan Walcott	Confess and you shall be spared.
Thomas Putnam	Confess and you shall not hang.
Samuel Parris	Confess.
Jonathan Walcott	Confess.
Thomas Putnam	Confess.

The men speak together.

Samuel Parris
Jonathan Walcott } Confess!
Thomas Putnam

Tituba speaks to the audience.

Tituba   They take me to prison. They lock me in the dark. I sit in chains. It is cold. There are rats. The Devil's creatures. He comes to me. He stands above me. A tall man in a black coat. He questions me. Again and again. He will have me confess. You are a witch. Say it. Confess. I try to speak. I cannot. Something grips my throat. A yellow snake. His voice in the dark. Confess. Say it. You are a witch. Confess and you shall be saved. Confess and you shall not die. Is this waking or dream? I cannot tell. Waking and dream. Their dream, their nightmare, and they have made it mine. Say it. Yes. Do you confess? Yes, yes, I am a witch, yes. I ride through the air, I dance in the woods. Are you alone? No. Are there others? Yes. I see them, they are here, I know their names. Sarah Good, you are one. Your daughter another. And more, more! They fly through the air, they dance in the woods. All doomed! All damned! All witches here in Salem!

ACT 3: THE DEVIL'S BOOK

● ●

SCENE 1

	The meeting house. **Sarah Good's** *examination.* **Sarah** *stands centre stage. Around and behind her, the* **Chorus** *stand. The three magistrates,* **John Hathorne, Nicholas Noyes,** *and* **Jonathan Corwin,** *are positioned in a small group to her left. To her right in another group are the afflicted girls –* **Betty Parris, Abigail Williams, Ann Putnam, Mercy Lewis,** *and* **Mary Walcott.** *Standing to one side, apart, is* **Mary Warren,** *observing.* **The magistrates** *question* **Sarah.**
John Hathorne	Sarah Good, why do you hurt these children?
Sarah Good	I do not hurt them.
Nicholas Noyes	Who do you employ to hurt them?
Sarah Good	I employ no one.
Jonathan Corwin	What creature do you employ?
Sarah Good	I employ no creature. I am falsely accused.
	The afflicted girls *cry out. They do to themselves what they say* **Sarah Good** *does.*
Betty Parris	She pinches my flesh! She pulls at my hair!
Abigail Williams	She grips my throat with her hands! She chokes me!
Ann Putnam	She scratches my face with her long nails!
Mercy Lewis	She freezes my body! I cannot move!
Mary Walcott	She bites me! See the marks on my arm!
John Hathorne	Do you see what you have done?
Nicholas Noyes	Why do you not tell us the truth?
Jonathan Corwin	Why do you torment these children?

Sarah Good	I do not torment them.

The girls cry out again, at the same time, over and over again. The magistrates shout over the noise. Sarah Good grows more and more frightened and desperate.

John Hathorne	Then who torments them?
Sarah Good	I cannot say.
Nicholas Noyes	How came they to be tormented?
Sarah Good	What do I know?
Jonathan Corwin	Who is it that torments these children?

Sarah looks on in terror as the girls continue to cry out. She calls above them.

Sarah Good	I cannot tell –
John Hathorne	Cannot, or will not?
Nicholas Noyes	You can, you must.
Jonathan Corwin	You must, and you shall!

Sarah breaks down.

Sarah Good	Very well – ! If I must tell I will tell –
John Hathorne	Tell us, then.
Nicholas Noyes	Tell us!
Jonathan Corwin	Tell us!

The girls suddenly fall silent. All watch Sarah Good in expectation. At last, she speaks.

Sarah Good	There are others here. Others who have made a pledge with the Devil. Here, in this meeting house. Here, among us. Others who have signed the Devil's book.
John Hathorne	Others?
Nicholas Noyes	Who are they?

Jonathan Corwin	What are the names of these others?
Sarah Good	They are all known to you.
	The girls cry out.
Betty Parris	Bridget Bishop!
Abigail Williams	Martha Corey!
Ann Putnam	Rebecca Nurse!
Mercy Lewis	Mary Easty!
Mary Walcott	Sarah Cloyce!
	Parris, Putnam, and Walcott come forward. They speak to the gathering.
Jonathan Walcott	It's as we told you. Our town is bewitched!
Samuel Parris	Here is proof! There are witches among us!
Thomas Putnam	And the Devil's abroad in Salem Village!
	The Chorus speak.
Chorus	Oh, the Devil's abroad in Salem He comes to afflict us He comes to haunt us He comes to trick us He comes to torment us Yes, the Devil's abroad in Salem.
	From the Chorus a witness steps forward.
1st Witness	I saw Sarah Good in my chamber. She carried a strange light. The air was close and I could not breathe. When I struck out at her, she vanished away.
Chorus	Yes, the Devil's abroad in Salem Here to make havoc In our town Here to strike The righteous down Oh, the Devil's abroad in Salem.

A second witness comes forward.

2nd Witness   I was returning home when in the dusk I saw a strange beast lying on the ground. I cannot say what it was. As I approached, it vanished, and two or three women stood in its place. When they saw me they fled into the air.

Chorus   Oh, the Devil's abroad in Salem
With lust and pride
He steals our souls
And opens wide
The gates of hell
Yes, the Devil's abroad in Salem.

*A **third witness** comes forward.*

3rd Witness   There was a light burning in a locked room. When I unlocked the door a large cat ran out. Later, Rebecca Nurse appeared to me and threatened to kill me if I told what I had seen.

Chorus   Yes, the Devil's abroad in Salem
He holds his hand
Before our eyes
And fills our hearts and minds
With lies.
Oh, the Devil's abroad in Salem
Yes, the Devil's abroad in Salem.

*Parris speaks to **all**.*

Samuel Parris   You have heard the witnesses. You have seen the afflictions put upon these poor children. Can there be further doubt? The evidence is here before us. Evil is at work. We must root it out, and we must destroy it. And all those who practise this evil, all those among us that have given their souls to wickedness, no matter who they may be, we shall not rest until we have found out their names, and cried out upon them all.

Betty cries out.

Betty Parris   I cry out upon Bridget Bishop!

*Mary Warren speaks to the audience. As she does so, she gradually comes in closer towards **the afflicted girls**.*

Mary Warren	I stand in the meeting house, one among those gathered. I am Mary Warren, servant to John and Elizabeth Proctor, and I have taken leave to attend these hearings.

Abigail cries out.

Abigail Williams	I cry out upon Martha Corey!
Mary Warren	I see these girls that I know, I see them afflicted, how their bodies twist, I hear their voices cry out upon those that afflict them.

Ann cries out.

Ann Putnam	I cry out upon Rebecca Nurse!
Mary Warren	And I see how they are all admired, how all hang upon their words, how the great of this land hear them and take heed of what they say.

Mercy Lewis cries out.

Mercy Lewis	I cry out upon Mary Easty!
Mary Warren	And I feel how they burn, the flame that runs in their blood, how their souls are on fire with authority and power.

Mary Walcott cries out.

Mary Walcott	I cry out upon Sarah Cloyce!
Mary Warren	And that same fire burns in me, it sears my skin, my blood jumps with its spark, and a voice of flame cries out in my head. And I give tongue to that voice, and I am also afflicted, and I cry out, I cry out on she who afflicts me!

The magistrates speak to Mary Warren.

John Hathorne	You, Mary Warren?
Nicholas Noyes	Whom do you cry out upon?
Jonathan Corwin	Who is it that afflicts you?

ACT 3 • SCENE 1

67

Mary Warren	Abigail Hobbs! I cry out upon Abigail Hobbs!

All are still but remain onstage.

• •

SCENE 2

*Salem Village. **Francis Nurse**, **Isaac Easty**, and **Peter Cloyce** enter.*

Francis Nurse	What can we do? These children are believed whomever they accuse.
Isaac Easty	Accusation is not judgement.
Peter Cloyce	What we witnessed today seemed like judgement to me.
Isaac Easty	There will be a trial. By then this madness will be over, and clearer minds shall judge them.
Francis Nurse	Meanwhile our wives are chained in Salem gaol.
Peter Cloyce	When I think of it – my Sarah – Rebecca and Mary – accused of this and made a public show –
Isaac Easty	We'll write a petition to the governor – and others – men of standing and authority –
Peter Cloyce	But will they heed it?
Isaac Easty	We are men of name and character –

Joseph Putnam and John Proctor enter.

Joseph Putnam	And it's those names that do condemn you.
Isaac Easty	I said it! That's what's at the bottom of all this. Our names!
John Proctor	These must be evil times when people are accused for the names they bear.
Peter Cloyce	So they are, John Proctor – and for all those who oppose Parris and Putnam and their clan.
John Proctor	There's no more to it than this?
Isaac Easty	Oh, there's more. Francis Nurse here has land Thomas Putnam claims is his. As do others who are named by these mouthing puppets.
Peter Cloyce	None are safe from Parris and Putnam now. For they have both God and the Devil working for them.
John Proctor	Joseph, do you believe it's your brother moves these girls to make their accusations?
Joseph Putnam	I do. He and Parris between them. Their girls were the first to be afflicted.
John Proctor	Then it's all manufacture –
Isaac Easty	Manufacture and fabrication and falsehood, yes! Malice and envy. Those are the diseases these children suffer.
Peter Cloyce	And it's a catching illness, sure. There's more fall to the malady each day. And not just children, grown women too.
Francis Nurse	Your serving-girl was one of them today, John Proctor.
Peter Cloyce	She was. She was taken in a fit and cried out she was afflicted.
Isaac Easty	Most convincing it was. I nearly believed her play-acting myself.
John Proctor	I'm sorry for it. I did not know she had gone there. But she'll not go there again. By tomorrow she'll be cured of her affliction.

Francis Nurse	It was not play-acting.
Joseph Putnam	What's that you say, Francis?
Francis Nurse	Neither Mary Warren nor the others. They did not play their fits.
Peter Cloyce	Do you say their fits are real?
Francis Nurse	Could anyone manufacture such torments as we saw today?
Joseph Putnam	Yes, I believe they could.
Isaac Easty	And I believe they did, and their trickery shall be exposed –
Francis Nurse	There may be trickery, yes, but there's more than that at work.
John Proctor	Do you mean witchcraft, Francis?
Peter Cloyce	You say the girls speak true, and our wives are witches?
Francis Nurse	No. I know that they are not. Nor any of those that are accused. But call it witchcraft or some other name, there is a power at work here. I saw it working in the meeting house today. And felt a touch of it myself.
Peter Cloyce	It is the Devil.
Francis Nurse	That may be a name to put to it. Though I think it has no name. It's something deep, beyond our understanding.
John Proctor	I say there's more of devilment than Devil at work here, and a good sound thrashing would put an end to all this wicked foolery. And so, good day to you.
	John Proctor goes.
Joseph Putnam	He may be right – but he should take care of making such views known. These are not times for open talk, and a rope's end will silence it.
	Joseph Putnam goes.
Peter Cloyce	He speaks the truth. We must be close with our thoughts.
Francis Nurse	But still we must do something to clear our good wives' names.

Isaac Easty	Then as I said, we'll put those thoughts on paper, and fold them close, and send them off to Boston. They are educated men there, and shall see the truth when it's put to them.
	Isaac Easty, Peter Cloyce, and Francis Nurse go.

●●●

SCENE 3

The woods near Salem, night. Mary Warren enters.

Mary Warren	I fear to go home. I know my master will have heard about my antics today, and will give me a beating for it. And perhaps it's right he should. I do not rightly know what happened at the meeting house, nor why I did cry out. It was as if there were some other within me. But if I speak that, they'll say I am possessed, a creature of the Devil. I'll be accused and cried out upon myself. What shall I do, then? Run away, perhaps. And go where? I have no family other than my master's, no home other than Salem. So I must stay, and find a way to face out what will come.
	Abigail Hobbs enters.
Abigail Hobbs	Is he here?
Mary Warren	Who's that?
Abigail Hobbs	Have you seen him?
Mary Warren	Abigail Hobbs –
Abigail Hobbs	He said he would be here, if I had need of him.
Mary Warren	Who do you mean?
Abigail Hobbs	It was here I first met him, in the woods. There were others but he chose me. There was music and we danced. He was tall and wore a black coat, his hair was white and his face was kind. But fearful also. And then he said I must sign his book and if I did he would help me if I had need, and so I signed it, and I have need but he is not here, and they pursue me.

71

Mary Warren	Who pursue you?
Abigail Hobbs	Men. But they shall not take me. I will send snakes and spiders to torment them, and a toad to drink their blood, and I shall fly into the air where they shall not find me.
Mary Warren	You have no such power –
Abigail Hobbs	Do you dare deny me? I signed his book and he gave me power –
Mary Warren	There is no such book and there is no such man!
Abigail Hobbs	And now you deny him – !
Mary Warren	You are a poor crazed girl, Abigail Hobbs, and all the village knows it.
Abigail Hobbs	Oh, Mary Warren, he will come to you at night and tear your soul, and then you'll know and fear him –

The Sheriff and his Assistant enter.

Sheriff	Abigail Hobbs.

Abigail swings round to face them.

We have you now, and there's no use you running more. You must come with us.

Abigail Hobbs	Who are you that I must go with you?
Sheriff	You know me. I am the Sheriff come to take you for questioning by the magistrates.
Abigail Hobbs	Bring them here to the woods and my master shall question them!
Sheriff's Assistant	Your master? And who might that be?
Abigail Hobbs	The Lord of the wood and the wild things!
Sheriff	Take her.
Abigail Hobbs	No!
Sheriff's Assistant	*[To Abigail]* Come on.

*The **Sheriff's Assistant** lays hands on **Abigail Hobbs**. She grabs his hand and sinks her teeth into it. He cries out.*

She bit me!

Sheriff   *[To **Abigail**]* You'll take a beating for that!

*The **Sheriff** raises his hand to strike **Abigail**. She falls to her knees.*

Abigail Hobbs   Oh, please don't beat me, mister! I mean no harm. Don't hurt me!

Sheriff   On your feet. *[he pulls her to her feet]* You mean no harm. I suppose you meant no harm when you sent your spirit to afflict this poor girl here.

Abigail Hobbs   I afflict her? Mary Warren? *[she laughs]* Who says so?

Sheriff   She does herself. She named you at the meeting house today.

Abigail Hobbs   Named me?

Sheriff's Assistant   As a foul witch who torments her soul. I was there. I heard her say it.

*Abigail turns and stares at **Mary**.*

Abigail Hobbs   She says so, does she? Well, then, take me! Let them question me! Yes! I shall tell! And I shall tell and name them all!

Sheriff   *[To his **Assistant**]* Bring her away.

Sheriff's Assistant   Come, witch, you're for prison, and there you'll lie in chains with all the rest until you're sent for.

*The **Sheriff** and his **Assistant** take **Abigail Hobbs** off. **Mary Warren** calls after them.*

Mary Warren   I did not mean it – I mean – I did not know what it was I said – I was in a fit – I – no – it was no fit – I know it – I saw the others – I acted as they acted – acting, yes, that's what it is – I did dissemble – and not I alone – for the others – all of them – they did dissemble too!

Mary remains onstage.

SCENE 4

*The meeting house, some days later. All are assembled – **the magistrates, the afflicted girls,** the Chorus. **The magistrates** are questioning **Mary Warren**. The movement to this scene from the last one is immediate and without break, so that it appears that **the magistrates** are responding to **Mary's** final words in the previous scene.*

John Hathorne   This is a serious accusation, Mary Warren.

Mary Warren turns to face the magistrates.

Nicholas Noyes   An accusation that may have serious consequences, for yourself and others.

Jonathan Corwin   Are you aware of what it is you are saying?

Mary Warren   I am, sir.

John Hathorne   That when you were here in the meeting house the other day you did purposely mislead this hearing.

Mary Warren   No, sir, I did not mislead –

Nicholas Noyes   But you have said that your affliction here the other day was pretence.

Mary Warren   I did not mean to –

Jonathan Corwin   What did you not mean to do? Mislead us, or pretend?

Mary Warren   I intended no deception –

John Hathorne   Yet you did deceive, whether purposely or not.

Nicholas Noyes   Or so you claim.

Jonathan Corwin   And further claim that these others also do deceive.

Mary Warren   I do not say that they deceive –

John Hathorne   You say they dissemble.

Nicholas Noyes   Is that not the same?

Jonathan Corwin	If they dissemble do they not also deceive?
Mary Warren	I don't know – I cannot say – I mean –
John Hathorne	It seems to us that you do not know what you mean.
Nicholas Noyes	Unless you mean mischief.
Jonathan Corwin	Do you come to this court to cause mischief, Mary Warren?
Mary Warren	No, sirs – I do not – I intend no harm to anyone –
John Hathorne	Then what do you intend?
Mary Warren	To tell –
Nicholas Noyes	To tell what?
Mary Warren	What I know –
Jonathan Corwin	And what is it that you know?
Mary Warren	The truth – I will tell the truth –
John Hathorne	It seems to us you do not know what the truth is.
Nicholas Noyes	Either you lied when you dissembled, or you lie now in claiming that you did.
Jonathan Corwin	Either way you bring falsehood to these hearings.
	The girls call out.
Betty Parris	Yes! She lies!
Abigail Williams	She is false!
Ann Putnam	All she says is falsehood!
Mercy Lewis	Trickery and deception!
Mary Walcott	She speaks with the Devil's tongue!
John Hathorne	Well, Mary Warren? How do you answer this?
Nicholas Noyes	Is it you that speaks falsehood or they?
Jonathan Corwin	Come! You have been charged! You must speak!
	The girls call out.

ACT 3 SCENE 4

Betty Parris	She cannot! They have stopped her mouth!
John Hathorne	Who has?
Abigail Williams	The spirits that attend her!
Nicholas Noyes	There are spirits?
Ann Putnam	Yes! We see them! And they torment us!
Jonathan Corwin	Whose spirits are they?
Mercy Lewis	The spirits of her master and mistress!
Mary Walcott	Goodman and Goodwife Proctor! There they sit grinning on the beam above!

*The magistrates speak to **Mary Warren**.*

John Hathorne	Is this true? Are their spirits here?
Mary Warren	I do not see them –
Nicholas Noyes	Then who torments these girls?
Mary Warren	I don't know –
Jonathan Corwin	Is it you, perhaps?
Mary Warren	No – I torment no one –
John Hathorne	Someone afflicts them!
Nicholas Noyes	Who is it?
Jonathan Corwin	Answer!
Mary Warren	I cannot – I know not how to answer –
John Hathorne	Then you must learn.
Nicholas Noyes	You will answer and you must!
Jonathan Corwin	Sheriff, take her into custody.
John Hathorne	Some time in gaol may teach her how to speak.
Nicholas Noyes	And send your men to Proctor's house. Bring Proctor and his wife.

Jonathan Corwin	They have been charged and must answer for it.
	*The **Sheriff** approaches **Mary Warren**.*
Sheriff	Come with me. *[she stares at him in terror]* Come! *[he grabs her by the arm and leads her off]*
	***All** remain onstage, still.*

• •

SCENE 5

*Salem Village, some time later. **Francis Nurse**, **Isaac Easty**, and **Peter Cloyce** enter.*

Francis Nurse	So John Proctor and his wife are taken.
Isaac Easty	And she with child. That at least will save her from the rope.
Peter Cloyce	Will it come to that?
Isaac Easty	It will, if he does not confess.
Francis Nurse	And he will not. He was ever a man for true and plain speaking.
Isaac Easty	And that's the cause he's named and taken, and his wife and servant with him.
Peter Cloyce	For speaking out against this madness, you mean?

Isaac Easty	I do. And madness it is when those that confess are spared and those that profess their innocence shall be hanged!
Francis Nurse	Don't raise your voice so, Isaac. If we will live to save our wives, we'd best keep our tongues locked and give our thoughts no voice.
Peter Cloyce	As to our wives, have you heard yet, Isaac, anything of the petition we sent?
Isaac Easty	No. Nothing. And I don't believe we shall. We are alone here, and surrounded by wolves and scoundrels –
Francis Nurse	No more of that, Isaac. See.
	*He nods towards **Samuel Parris** and **Thomas Putnam**, who are approaching them.*
Samuel Parris	Good day to you, sirs.
	*The three men nod to **Parris** but do not speak to him.*
Thomas Putnam	What's this? Do you not acknowledge your Minister?
Isaac Easty	We see he's here.
Thomas Putnam	But you don't deign to speak to him.
Isaac Easty	I'll speak to him, and to you –
Francis Nurse	Good day to you, Mr Parris.
Peter Cloyce	And to you, Thomas Putnam.
Samuel Parris	I'm glad we've met. I've been meaning to speak with you. I do not see you at church of late. Your absence is most remiss. All those brethren who mean well by this community would do well to attend. Their prayers are needed at this time. The church is your armour, gentlemen, against the assailments of the Devil, which are strong at this time. I hope to see you there. And if not, to know your reasons.
Isaac Easty	If we have reasons for not attending, you shall know them shortly!
Samuel Parris	Well, then, Isaac Easty. So I shall. Good day to you again.

Samuel Parris goes.

Thomas Putnam   And I hope your reasons, whatever they may be, are firm and sound. Good day.

Thomas Putnam goes.

Isaac Easty   Our reasons! We have reason enough with our womenfolk chained in prison! I'll give him reason!

Francis Nurse   In due course we all shall, Isaac. But not now.

Peter Cloyce   The man has no heart. To say such things. To ask us our reasons. He can have no heart.

Isaac Easty   You're right, Peter Cloyce. He doesn't. And neither do I. For what heart I once had has been torn out of me.

Francis Nurse, Peter Cloyce, and Isaac Easty go.

SCENE 6

*The gaol. The **Chorus** speak as **Mary Warren** enters slowly centre stage.*

Chorus
Salem's a prison
Where the innocent weep
A place of privation
A place of horror
A dungeon dug deep
In the dark earth
Where the dank walls drip with filthy water
And rats' claws scratch on broken stones.

Mary Warren speaks to herself.

Mary Warren   This is not real. It cannot be real. There can be no place like this. It is a dream, a bad dream, yes, and I shall wake from it. I shall close my eyes and count, and when I have counted I shall wake.

*She shuts her eyes. The **Chorus** speak.*

Chorus	Salem's a prison Where the innocent are damned A place of torment A place of torture Chained to its walls They cannot move And their torment continues And it has no end.

Mary Warren opens her eyes and stares around in horror.

Mary Warren	No! It is no dream. But I have done nothing wrong! I have committed no crime! I should not be here! *[she calls out]* Unlock the door! Let me out of here! You must let me out!

The Chorus speak.

Chorus	Salem's a prison Where innocence dies In a filthy corner Wrapped in rags It shivers and starves And stares into the dark Beyond weeping, beyond torment Lost to the world, beyond hope.

Mary Warren	*[Resigned to her fate]* They do not let me out. The door remains locked. This is no dream. I shall not wake. I am Mary Warren and have been accused of witchcraft, and unless I confess, I shall stay in this place until they come to hang me.

The Chorus have moved apart to reveal Dorcas Good. She sits on the floor, hands wrapped around her knees, and rocks backwards and forwards in a repetitive motion. She chants softly to herself as she rocks.

Dorcas Good	A tall man in a black coat, a tall man in a black coat, a tall man in a black coat, a tall man in a black coat ... *etc.*

Mary Warren sees her and crosses to her as Dorcas continues to chant.

| Mary Warren | Dorcas Good? Are you here? A little child. They would name you a witch as well. Dorcas. Do you know me? I am Mary Warren. Sometimes I gave you bread when you came begging for it. And once I gave you some buttons for playthings. Dorcas Good? Do you hear me? |

*All this time **Dorcas** has kept up her rocking and chanting. Now, **Mary Warren** touches her on the shoulder, and **Dorcas** stops abruptly, with a start and gasp, and looks at **Mary**.*

Dorcas Good	I did not steal it.
Mary Warren	What?
Dorcas Good	I was give it. She give it me but they will not believe me, so they have put me here. And she tried to tell them I did not steal it but they would not believe her so she is here as well.
Mary Warren	Who is here?
Dorcas Good	Goody Nurse. Ask her, she will tell you I did not steal it.
Mary Warren	I know you didn't.
Dorcas Good	Then tell them. Will you tell them? If you tell them they will believe you and they will let me out. I don't like it here. It's dark and it is cold and I am afraid. Will you help me?
Mary Warren	I don't think I can –

Dorcas Good	Please, you must help me, I have done nothing wrong, I did not steal it, she give it me, and if you tell them they will listen, please, please, tell them, tell them, tell them.

Other characters now speak from the Chorus. Mary Warren reacts to them all as they speak.

Sarah Good	Tell them.
Rebecca Nurse	Tell them what you know.
Sarah Cloyce	Tell them the truth.
Mary Easty	Speak, and they will listen.
John Proctor	Speak and you will save us.
Mary Warren	Save you – ?
John Proctor	You know we are no witches, Mary Warren.
Mary Easty	You know we bear no guilt.
Sarah Cloyce	We are all of us innocent.
Rebecca Nurse	But our innocence will not save us.
Sarah Good	Only you can save us.
Dorcas Good	Save us, Mary Warren, save us, save us, save us, save us, save us, save us . . . *etc.*

Dorcas rocks backwards and forwards repeating her words over and over. Disturbed and upset, Mary Warren backs away from her.

Mary Warren	I cannot – I cannot save you – I cannot even save myself –

Samuel Parris enters.

Samuel Parris	But you can.

Mary Warren turns to face Samuel Parris.

You can save yourself, child. If you confess. Confess that you gave yourself to the Devil, confess to this pernicious sin, and that sin shall be forgiven, and your soul saved.

Mary Warren	But I did not – I have not –

Samuel Parris	You have been accused!
Mary Warren	They are false –
Samuel Parris	It is you that are false, by your own admission!
Mary Warren	I have committed no sin –
Samuel Parris	All are sinners, Mary Warren, and all shall be forgiven if they confess those sins. Yet if they do not, and take that sin with them beyond the grave, then shall the torments of hell await them.
Mary Warren	I do not want to die –
Samuel Parris	And you shall not, if you confess, and if you name those that brought you this sin.
Mary Warren	I do not know who you mean –
	Thomas Putnam enters.
Thomas Putnam	We mean John Proctor and his wife.
	Mary Warren turns to Thomas Putnam.
	It was they who brought you to the Devil. Say it.
Mary Warren	I cannot –
Thomas Putnam	They are foul witches. Say it.
Mary Warren	I must not –
Thomas Putnam	Cannot? Must not? Will not? Then must you be condemned with all the rest. And hang alongside them too.
Mary Warren	No – !
Thomas Putnam	It's a bad death to hang at a rope's end. To feel the noose about your neck. To drop and kick and dance in air.
Samuel Parris	And to feel the Devil pulling at your heels. Pulling the life out of your body, Mary Warren, and your soul as well. And once he has that soul, he has it for eternity, and there's nought but suffering and pain and torment and no relief or pity for your agonies.
Thomas Putnam	Unless you do confess.

ACT 3   SCENE 6

Samuel Parris	Confess, and be saved.
Thomas Putnam	Confess, and be spared.
Samuel Parris	You must.
Thomas Putnam	You will.
Samuel Parris	Confess.
Thomas Putnam	Confess!

In terror and desperation Mary Warren cries out.

Mary Warren	Very well! I do confess! Yes! I confess!

Mary stops. She composes herself, gains control, and walks forward. Then she speaks calmly to the audience.

I signed the Devil's book. It was my master brought me to it. And my mistress. They said they would torment me if I did not sign. Both are foul witches. And so are the others named. Foul witches, all of them. They took me to their gathering in the woods, and there was music played, and they did dance, and I danced with my master, and my mistress looked on and laughed. And then he made me kneel and gave me a book to sign and said it was the Devil's book, and I must sign my name, and I did, for fear of him. Then we feasted and drank blood and all bowed down before my master for he is a great wizard and master of all the witches here in Salem. And I will name them. John and Elizabeth Proctor, Rebecca Nurse and Sarah Cloyce, Mary Easty, Abigail Hobbs, Sarah Good and Dorcas Good her daughter, and others I shall name hereafter, foul witches that do afflict us all.

Pause.

And I am Mary Warren, and I do confess, and send them to their graves that are innocent. And so I lose my soul.

She bows her head.

All are still onstage.

End of Act 3

EPILOGUE

Gallows Hill.

*The **Chorus** speak to the audience.*

Chorus
This is Mary Warren
And this is her dream
Her dream and her nightmare
From which she can't wake
And it's our dream too
That holds us fast
All of us trapped in the same bad dream
Where we stand in a crowd below Gallows Hill
Gazing up at the tree where the ladder stands
And the rope hangs
And the neck's in the noose
And the body drops
And legs kick in the strangling air
Again and again
Again and again
And though they are all gone under the ground
And though we too are gone under the ground
Still it holds us fast
And keeps us here
The bad dream
The nightmare from which we can't wake.

Mary Warren looks up.

Mary Warren
Now I will tell. I will confess. We did but dissemble.

85

Activities

Year 8

Key Stage 3 Framework Objectives	Relevant Activities Chapter(s)
Word Level	
14 Language change	Writing a Formal Appeal
Sentence Level	
13 Change over time	Writing a Formal Appeal
Reading	
1 Combine information	Features of Playscripts
3 Notemaking formats	Presenting Facts; Features of Playscripts; Insiders and Outsiders
4 Versatile reading	Tituba
5 Trace developments	Presenting Facts; Features of Playscripts; Insiders and Outsiders; The Power of Speech; Tituba
7 Implied and explicit meanings	Insiders and Outsiders; The Power of Speech; Tituba
10 Development of key ideas	Presenting Facts; Features of Playscripts; Insiders and Outsiders; The Power of Speech
13 Interpret a text	Insiders and Outsiders; The Power of Speech
14 Literary conventions	Features of Playscripts; The Power of Speech
16 Cultural context	The Power of Speech; Tituba
Writing	
1 Effective planning	Writing a Formal Appeal; The Power of Speech; Reporting on the Salem Witch Trials
2 Anticipate reader reaction	Writing a Formal Appeal; The Power of Speech
3 Writing to reflect	Features of Playscripts
7 Establish the tone	The Power of Speech
10 Effective information	Reporting on the Salem Witch Trials
11 Explain complex ideas	Reporting on the Salem Witch Trials
13 Present a case persuasively	Writing a Formal Appeal
14 Develop an argument	Writing a Formal Appeal
16 Balanced analysis	Reporting on the Salem Witch Trials
17 Integrate evidence	Reporting on the Salem Witch Trials
18 Critical review	Features of Playscripts
Speaking and Listening	
1 Evaluate own speaking	Presenting Facts; Features of Playscripts; Insiders and Outsiders; The Power of Speech; Reporting on the Salem Witch Trials
3 Formal presentation	Presenting Facts; Reporting on the Salem Witch Trials

Key Stage 3 Framework Objectives	Relevant Activities Chapter(s)
5 Questions to clarify	Insiders and Outsiders
7 Listen for specific purpose	Presenting Facts
8 Hidden messages	Features of Playscripts; The Power of Speech
9 Evaluate own contributions	Features of Playscripts; Insiders and Outsiders; The Power of Speech; Tituba; Reporting on the Salem Witch Trials
10 Hypothesis and speculation	Insiders and Outsiders; Tituba
11 Building on others	Presenting Facts; Features of Playscripts; Insiders and Outsiders; The Power of Speech; Tituba; Reporting on the Salem Witch Trials
12 Varied roles in discussion	Reporting on the Salem Witch Trials
Drama	
13 Evaluate own drama skills	Insiders and Outsiders; The Power of Speech; Tituba
14 Dramatic techniques	Features of Playscripts; Insiders and Outsiders; The Power of Speech; Tituba
15 Work in role	Insiders and Outsiders; Tituba
16 Collaborative presentation	Presenting Facts; Features of Playscripts; Insiders and Outsiders; The Power of Speech; Tituba; Reporting on the Salem Witch Trials

SALEM ACTIVITIES

Year 9

Key Stage 3 Framework Objectives	Relevant Activities Chapter(s)
Sentence Level	
3 Degrees of formality	Writing a Formal Appeal
9 Sustained Standard English	Writing a Formal Appeal
11 Trends over time	Writing a Formal Appeal
Reading	
1 Information retrieval	Features of Playscripts; Tituba
3 Notemaking at speed	Presenting Facts; Features of Playscripts; Writing a Formal Appeal; Tituba
12 Rhetorical devices	Features of Playscripts; Insiders and Outsiders; Writing a Formal Appeal; The Power of Speech; Tituba
14 Analyse scenes	Features of Playscripts; Insiders and Outsiders; The Power of Speech
Writing	
2 Exploratory writing	Features of Playscripts; Writing a Formal Appeal; Reporting on the Salem Witch Trials
5 Narrative techniques	Features of Playscripts
9 Integrate information	Writing a Formal Appeal
11 Descriptive detail	Reporting on the Salem Witch Trials
13 Influence audience	Writing a Formal Appeal; The Power of Speech
Speaking and Listening	
1 Evaluate own talk	Presenting Facts; Features of Playscripts; Insiders and Outsiders; The Power of Speech; Reporting on the Salem Witch Trials
2 Standard English	Presenting Facts; Features of Playscripts; Reporting on the Salem Witch Trials
3 Interview techniques	Tituba; Reporting on the Salem Witch Trials
4 Evaluate listening skills	Presenting Facts; Features of Playscripts; Insiders and Outsiders; The Power of Speech
7 Identify underlying issues	Insiders and Outsiders; Reporting on the Salem Witch Trials
8 Evaluate own contributions	Insiders and Outsiders; Tituba; Reporting on the Salem Witch Trials
9 Considered viewpoint	Features of Playscripts; Insiders and Outsiders; The Power of Speech; Tituba
10 Group organization	Presenting Facts; Insiders and Outsiders; Reporting on the Salem Witch Trials

Key Stage 3 Framework Objectives	Relevant Activities Chapter(s)
Drama	
11 Evaluate own drama skills	Features of Playscripts; Insiders and Outsiders; The Power of Speech; Tituba; Reporting on the Salem Witch Trials
12 Drama techniques	Features of Playscripts; Insiders and Outsiders; The Power of Speech; Tituba; Reporting on the Salem Witch Trials
14 Convey character and atmosphere	Features of Playscripts; Insiders and Outsiders; The Power of Speech
15 Critical evaluation	Reporting on the Salem Witch Trials

Presenting Facts

The play *Salem* is based on real events. Here are some facts about those events. They are in a random order.

In 1626, a colony of Puritans settled in Salem, New England.

The women were told that they would be hanged unless they confessed and named other witches.

In May 1693, all those still accused in gaol were released.

People suspected that the girls had been bewitched. They were encouraged to name the witches.

The settlers were farmers and tradesmen. Life was hard. Some had to fight off attacks from Native Americans.

Samuel Parris was not popular. He demanded a high salary, free firewood and cheap corn. In 1691 some villagers refused to pay his salary.

In 1689, the Reverend Samuel Parris became Minister in the Church of Salem Village.

In February 1692, nine-year-old Betty Parris, her cousin Abigail Williams and friend Ann Putnam began to have fits – screaming, shouting and shaking.

In October 2001, all those accused of witchcraft in the Salem trials were officially declared innocent.

The girls named Tituba (Parris' slave), Sarah Good and Sarah Osburn as witches. The accused women were sent to gaol then brought before judges.

In the summer of 1692, 19 innocent men and women were hanged for witchcraft in Salem. One man was pressed to death under heavy rocks for refusing to stand trial. Four people died in gaol as a result of the trial.

As people became more afraid, the witch-hunt grew. People accused each other in order to save themselves.

1   In pairs, put the facts in chronological order (the order in which they happened).
    Look carefully at:
    - the dates
    - the name links
    - the actions and their consequences.
2   Compare your results with those of another pair. If you disagree, explain your reasoning and decide, as a four, which is the correct order. One person in the group should note down the final order of events.
3   Divide up the facts between the group for presentation. No student should have consecutive facts to present.
4   Present the facts, with the group standing in a line. Each narrator steps forward to present their fact, then steps back. Do NOT stand in chronological order, but listen carefully to judge when your turn comes. In groups of four, each student will have three facts to present.

Remember!
- The group must remain still and silent except for the student who is speaking.
- The speaker should look directly at the audience and speak slowly and clearly.
- Practise your presentation to make it fluent and confident.

Assessment
- Self-assessment. Think carefully about your presentation skills. Rate them as either 'good', 'quite good' or 'could be better'.
- Peer assessment. Ask the class to comment on two good features of the presentation and one which could be improved. For example, they might consider how well the group worked together, how clearly they spoke, how loudly they spoke, and how still they were during the presentation.

Features of Playscripts

Most playscripts are written in a traditional way. They use features that readers and actors are familiar with. Some of the most common features are listed below.

1 Match up the features to their correct definitions. (Use a dictionary to look up any unfamiliar terms.)

Features	Definitions
Prologue	A group speaking or singing together
Act	One of the smaller divisions of a play (there are usually several Scenes in each Act)
Scene	One of the main divisions of a play
Chorus	A short section at the end of a play
Stage directions	Instructions about what an actor must do, often presented in italics
Epilogue	An introduction, found at the beginning of a play

Prologue

1 Reread the Prologue of *Salem*.
2 With a partner, talk about the effect of this Prologue on the audience. Consider the following questions:
   • Is it a gentle or dramatic opening?
   • Will the audience understand what is happening?
   • What emotions do the characters display?
   • What effect does the darkness have?
   • Can you pick out key words that sum up the atmosphere and mood?
   • How would you describe the role of the Chorus, as they chant 'Hang her...'?

3 Together, compose a short paragraph linking your ideas together. Start by stating what effect you think the Prologue might have on the audience and then go on to explain why, using evidence from the text.

4 Discuss the advantages and disadvantages of starting a play with this sort of scene. Jot down some notes, so you can share your ideas with the class.

Advantages	Disadvantages
It grabs the audience's attention	It gives away the ending
It sets the mood for . . .	It might confuse people because . . .

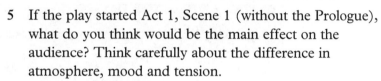

5 If the play started Act 1, Scene 1 (without the Prologue), what do you think would be the main effect on the audience? Think carefully about the difference in atmosphere, mood and tension.

6 Share your ideas with the rest of the class or group. If you can, suggest another starting point for the play, giving reasons for your choice.

Assessment

- Self-assessment. Decide how confident you are about understanding the key features of a playscript: 'very', 'fairly' or 'not really'. If you need to reinforce your understanding, look back through the features and find an example of each in *Salem*.

- Peer assessment. Ask your partner to name one skill that you used well and one that might need some improvement. They could consider: how well you listened to them; how clearly you shared your ideas; how easily you picked out key words; how imaginative you were at suggesting a new starting point for the play.

Chorus

The word 'chorus' comes from the Greek word *khoros*. It can be used as a verb or a noun, with many different meanings. Here are some of the meanings:

A large group of singers

A part of a song which is repeated after each verse

A single actor, or group, who speak the prologue and epilogue of a play

A device used with an amplified instrument to make it sound as if more instruments are being played

A group of dancers who move together

A group of actors who comment on the main action of a play. They often move and speak together

To speak or sing together (verb)

1   With a partner, think carefully about the Chorus in *Salem*. Decide which meanings above apply. Find examples to back up your decisions and note them down.
2   Share your thoughts with the rest of the group or class.
3   Talk about why a Chorus is useful to a playwright. Think carefully about:
   • volume
   • number of actors
   • tension
   • creating atmosphere.
4   David Calcutt uses the Chorus flexibly. He does not always make them speak or act together. Find two examples when one of the Chorus breaks away from the main group to say something independently. What effect does this have?
5   In groups, experiment with the different effects that can be created during the chanting 'Hang her, hang the witch!

Hang her, hang the witch! . . . *etc.*' Try varying the speed, volume and emphasis. Choose the style which you think has the most dramatic impact and perform it in front of the class.

Assessment
- The teacher can judge which performance has the most dramatic impact.

Insiders and Outsiders

When the four young girls, Betty Parris, Ann Putnam, Abigail Williams and Mercy Lewis were asked to name the people who were tormenting them, they accused three women of being witches: Tituba, Sarah Good, and Sarah Osburn.

Here are some notes about the three women:

Tituba
- the Parris family's slave
- an Indian, from South America
- owned by Mr Parris before he had his family
- as a slave, she had no money, rights or authority

Sarah Good
- daughter of a wealthy merchant who killed himself
- cheated out of her inheritance by her stepfather
- unhappily married to a man who would not work
- reduced to begging in the street
- did not go to church

Sarah Osburn
- an elderly, outspoken, unpopular woman
- married to her former servant
- did not go to church

In any community or group, some people stand out as being slightly different from the majority. They may have different interests, different backgrounds, different experiences or just a different attitude to life. (These people might find themselves to be in a majority in other groups.)

Some people dislike and fear anyone who appears to be different or vulnerable in some way. They may try to frighten and bully them.

1   In groups, discuss why the girls might have chosen these three women to accuse of witchcraft. Share your ideas as a group and note down two possible reasons why each woman was accused.

2   Each group should appoint a spokesperson to present the ideas to the rest of the class. After listening to all the spokespeople, decide, as a class, on the most likely reasons for each woman.

3   Each group should find a speech given by either Sarah Good (Act 2, Scene 1), or Tituba (Act 2, Scene 4), which they feel gives insight into the character's feelings and position in society. Copy out the speech and underline key phrases which reveal most about them.

4   Reread the scenes where the young girls bully Dorcas Good and Tituba. Note how they 'close in' on their victim, undermine them, insult them and try to frighten and control them.

5   In *Salem*, David Calcutt chose not to show the girls' relationship with Sarah Osburn. Imagine he has decided to add a scene, and asks you, as a group, to write it. Follow the steps below:

Step 1
Discuss what you know about Sarah Osburn and the young girls.

Step 2
Decide on a setting where the girls might come across Sarah and start talking to her. Remember, she was well-known for her bad temper, so she might have been easily irritated by them.

Step 3
Decide on how the girls might react – both verbally and physically.
Think carefully about why they might laugh at or criticize her.

Step 4
Choose a suitable way of ending the scene.

Step 5
After discussion, either improvise the scene or write it out as a script.
Perform it in front of the class.

Remember!
- The girls are young, but feel they are important in the community.
- They would have overheard adults gossiping about Sarah and her husband.
- Sarah Osburn was unconventional and elderly.

Assessment

- Self-assessment. Think about the contributions you made to the group discussions. Rate your performance out of ten for the following skills:
  - listening to other people
  - voicing your own ideas
  - helping the group to reach decisions.
- Teacher assessment. Ask your teacher for feedback on your performance or script. It is useful to know two aspects that you did well and one aspect that needs further work.

Writing a Formal Appeal

In Act 3, Scene 2, Isaac Easty suggests that the husbands of the accused women write a letter of appeal to the authorities in Boston. He says 'They are educated men there, and shall see the truth when it's put to them.'

Draft a formal letter to Sir William Phips, Governor of the colony, on behalf of Isaac Easty, Francis Nurse, and Peter Cloyce. Remember that they are appealing on behalf of their wives, Mary Easty, Rebecca Nurse, and Sarah Cloyce.

Work in pairs and follow the steps below.

Step 1
Make notes on exactly what you want to say. You need to give reasons for your appeal. Think about:
- Why you feel the trials are unfair
- What you feel about the girls' afflictions
- How you feel about the magistrates and judges
- Why those accused are confessing and naming other witches.

Step 2
Make notes about what you would like to happen. Think about:
- Asking the authorities to witness the trials
- Moving the trials out of Salem, to Boston
- Stopping the executions and freeing those in gaol.

Step 3
Before you draft your letter, think carefully about how to make it formal and give it authority. You need to use Standard English, which involves:
- Keeping the tenses consistent
- Avoiding dialect words or slang expressions
- Making sure the spelling and punctuation is correct
- Starting and finishing the letter with appropriate wording.

Step 4

Write a first draft of your letter. Give it to another pair to read. Ask them to suggest ways of improving your letter, and to point out what they feel are its strengths.

Step 5

Revise your letter, taking into account any comments that you feel are valuable. Proofread it to check for spelling and grammatical errors, then write out a final, neat version.

An historical letter

In July 1692, John Proctor was also accused of witchcraft and sent to Salem gaol to await trial. While waiting he sent a petition (letter of appeal) to the Boston authorities, asking for help. Here is an extract from that letter.

SALEM ACTIVITIES

> The innocency of our Case with the Enmity of our Accusers and our Judges, and Jury, whom nothing but our Innocent blood will serve their turn, having Condemned us already before our Tryals, being so much incensed and engaged against us by the Devil, makes us bold to Beg and Implore your Favourable Assistance of this our Humble Petition to his Excellency, That if it be possible our Innocent Blood may be spared, which undoubtedly otherwise will be shed, if the Lord doth not mercifully step in. The Magistrates, Ministers, Jewries, and all the People in general, being so much inraged and incensed against us by the Delusion of the Devil, which we can term no other, by reason we know in our own Consciences, we are all Innocent Persons.

A rough modern translation might be:

'Because we are innocent, and our accusers are so hostile (nothing less than our blood will satisfy them, and they condemned us as guilty even before our trial, were set against us by the Devil), we beg your help to spare our innocent blood. The magistrates and jury and others have been stirred

103

up by the false Devil, we can't explain it any other way because our consciences are clear, we are all innocent.'

John Proctor's letter was written over 300 years ago. Look carefully at the original version. How does it look different to modern writing? Think about:
- the use of capital letters
- the length of the sentences
- the different spellings
- unfamiliar words and phrases.

John Proctor's letter failed to help him. He was hanged on August 19th 1692.

The Power of Speech

The Reverend Samuel Parris is a powerful character in *Salem*. He is a great orator (speaker) and influences many people through his persuasive, dramatic prayers and sermons.

Look carefully at his prayer in Act 1, Scene 9.

'O, Lord, there are devils in Christ's church, Satan's brood dwelling here among us. They would tear down thy holy city, O, Lord, throw open its shining gates and let in hell. Thou knowest them, Lord, their faces to thee are not hidden. And with thy grace we shall know them also, and cry out upon them. Be they neighbour or friend, sister or brother, they are an abomination to the people of the Lord, and shall be cast out. O, Lord, lend us thy strength for this great task, that we may cleanse this village of infection, and crush our enemies, and let fall thy wrath upon their heads!'

1 Look carefully at some of the rhetorical devices that Parris uses. Find examples of:
   • the repetition of words and phrases
   • descriptions which conjure up powerful images
   • violent verbs (action words)
   • nouns which might trigger fear and horror.
2 In small groups, decide how this speech might be delivered for maximum effect. Think about:
   • what sort of reaction the speaker is trying to provoke in his audience
   • key words to emphasize
   • where pauses might be most effective
   • the use of volume (how it might increase and decrease).
3 Annotate a copy of the speech to show your decisions, e.g. underline words to be loud, insert vertical lines to show pauses, etc.

4   Choose one person in your group to deliver the prayer, using the techniques you have discussed. Practise the speech, with the rest of the group chanting the final lines, as in the playscript.

Assessment
Peer assessment: Ask your audience to comment on two things that your group did well and one thing that it could improve upon.

The rule of fear

When Samuel Parris sees Ann and Betty talking to Sarah Good, he is furious (Act 2, Scene 2). He lectures them on their duty to be obedient to their parents and to God. It is a speech intended to frighten them into obedience.

'Obedience is all. Our society stands by obedience. It falls by the lack of it. Was not disobedience the first sin? Was it not through disobedience that Adam fell and was cast out of Eden? It is a most grievous sin, this sin of disobedience, and it marks Man out for death. Death is our lot, it is the inheritance we have received from our first father, for his sin of disobedience. And death may strike us down at any time. Do you think that you are not marked out for death? Do you believe you are too young to die? Children! Go to the burying ground. There you will see many graves smaller than your own may be. They that lie in them were not too young to die. You are not too young to die. And when it comes, as come it will, are you prepared? Are your souls in readiness? Because if they are not you will be damned, and you will suffer for eternity the wretched pains and torments of hell!'

1   In pairs, decide how this speech would frighten the children. Think about:
    • where he tells them to go
    • what he says could happen to them very soon
    • what he says might be the consequences of them

dying if their souls are not 'ready' (i.e. if they have not behaved well).

Share your ideas with another pair.

2   This is a persuasive speech, intended to make the girls more obedient. What persuasive techniques does he use? Choose some of the techniques below and identify examples.

rhetorical questions (which do not require an answer)

imperatives (verbs which give commands)

repetition (to reinforce ideas and themes)

direct address (to get the attention of an audience)

short sentences (for impact)

strong images (to make the message clear and frighten the girls)

3   In pairs, write your own short persuasive speech, using some of the techniques above. Your speaker could be:
   • Samuel Parris, giving a sermon about the need for honesty or charity
   • A parent or teacher, persuading students to do their homework
   • A young person, persuading his or her friends to break one of the school rules.

4   Deliver your speech to another pair or to the class.

Remember!
• Vary the tone and volume of your voice for effect.
• Include pauses to add to the drama.
• Make eye contact with your audience.
• Use facial expressions and gestures to back up your speech.

Assessment

- Self-assessment. Give yourself marks out of ten for the way you worked with your partner. Think about how carefully you listened and combined your ideas.
- Teacher assessment. Ask your teacher to assess a) the content of your speech and b) its delivery.

Tituba

Tituba was the first person accused of being a witch by the girls and, later, she went on to accuse others.

What sort of woman was Tituba?

1 Read these extracts from the play. While you are reading, think carefully about how David Calcutt portrays Tituba.

'I may be a slave, but I am slave to Mr Parris. I work for my keep and am no beggar woman.'

'I am no heathen! I am Christian too!'

'They call my people savages, say we worship the Devil, and are devils ourselves. They say our hearts are wild and filled with darkness. But there are dark hearts beating in these folk too, and a fear and a wildness in their eyes. I've seen how they treat others of their kind, with beatings and with whippings and with hangings . . . it's a savage God they worship.'

'But I'm a slave and must be silent, until my masters bid me speak.'

'This is a bad dream. But it is not my dream. It is theirs. These children's, the people of this village. Their own nightmare story . . . But now they have made me a part of their story. I am walking into it out of the shadows.'

2 With a partner, read the statements below and decide whether they are **true** or **false**. Back up your decisions with evidence from the quotations above.
   • Tituba feels like an outsider.
   • Tituba has no pride.
   • Tituba is a disobedient slave.

- Tituba is intelligent and has her own opinions.
- Tituba is in control of her life.

Why does Tituba confess and accuse others?

In Act 2, Scene 6, some of the men are trying to work out what or who is responsible for their daughters' strange behaviour. Samuel Parris admits that he has questioned Tituba 'severely'. It is likely that she would have been whipped.

At the end of Act 2, the girls are urged to name the witch who torments them. They name Tituba. Samuel Parris, Jonathan Walcott, and Thomas Putnam urge Tituba to confess:

'Confess and you shall be saved.'
'Confess and you shall be spared.'
'Confess and you shall not hang.'

Tituba herself tells the audience what happened:

'They take me to prison. They lock me in the dark. I sit in chains. It is cold. There are rats . . . He stands above me . . . He questions me. Again and again. He will have me confess. You are a witch. Say it. Confess. I try to speak. I cannot . . . Confess and you shall be saved. Confess and you shall not die . . .'

By confessing early on and naming other witches, Tituba did not have to go to trial, but she remained in prison.

Historical evidence shows us that after the trials and executions, Tituba withdrew her confession (i.e. said that she was not a witch). Samuel Parris was so outraged at this that he refused to pay the prison fee of seven pounds for her release. Tituba remained in prison for over a year, until someone else bought her.

Interviewing Tituba

Imagine it is 1702, ten years after the Salem Witch Trials. Tituba is still alive, but working for a new master. Someone wants to know what happened at the Salem Witch Trials, so he or she goes to visit Tituba.

1   As a group or in pairs, draw up a list of questions that you might want to ask Tituba. Try to avoid questions which have just 'yes' or 'no' answers.
    • Ask about the sequence of events.
    • Find out how she felt at the time.
    • Decide whether her feelings have changed since then.
2   One person in the group should volunteer to take on the role of Tituba and be prepared to answer the questions. In preparation for the role, remember:
    • to stay in character throughout the interview
    • to think carefully about how an older woman might speak and move
    • that feelings can change over time.

Conduct the interview in front of the rest of the class. Invite more questions from the 'audience'. One of the audience might like to take on the role of another character, who may contradict some of what Tituba says!

Assessment
• Self-assessment. If you played the role of Tituba, give yourself marks out of five for:
  - staying in character
  - giving thoughtful, full replies to the questions
  - remembering the events accurately.
• Peer assessment. Ask the class to decide which were the two best questions that you asked. Ask them which question could have been changed a little to get a more interesting answer.

Reporting on the Salem Witch Trials

As a group, discuss, plan and present a television news report on the Salem Witch Trials. Imagine that the atmosphere of fear and suspicion is at its height, with the gaol in Salem filling up with more and more accused people.

Step 1
As a group, discuss how to structure your report. You might include:
- interviews with local people
- a summary of the situation to date
- some background detail about some of the accused
- quotations from the court
- speculation as to what might happen next
- visuals to aid your report, e.g. maps, photos of the village, sketches of court scenes.

Appoint someone to chair your discussion and someone else to note down decisions made.

Remember!
Take turns in speaking and be prepared to listen carefully to others.

Step 2
Divide up the project into separate tasks for pairs or individual members of the group to research and write.

Step 3
Draft and then finalize each section of the report.

Remember!
A news report should be balanced and fair, giving all sides of the story.

Step 4

Bring the group together again and look through the whole report. You may need to find ways of linking up the different aspects of the report. Decide who will present the report and who will take on the roles of interviewees.

Step 5

Present your report in front of the whole class.

Remember!
A presenter should stand still and look directly at the audience. He or she needs to speak clearly and concisely.

Assessment

- Self-assessment. Think carefully about how well you worked in the group. Ask yourself the following questions:
  - Did I contribute some ideas?
  - Did I express myself clearly?
  - Did I answer any questions that other people had?
  - Did I listen to other people's ideas?
  - Did I help the group make decisions?
- Teacher assessment. Ask the teacher to comment on your presentation. Ask him or her to highlight the strengths of your presentation and also to identify one area that could do with more work.

SALEM ACTIVITIES

Further activities

1 Write a diary entry for one of the characters in the play. Include details of events during the day, as well as thoughts and feelings about them.

2 Write or present a short sermon that Reverend Samuel Parris might have preached during the Salem Witch Trials. Think carefully about his views and the way that he expresses them in the play.

3 Look up the meaning of the word 'witch-hunt' in a dictionary. Another play about the Salem Witch Trials is *The Crucible*, written in 1953 by Arthur Miller. He wrote it at a time when he believed there was a witch-hunt going on in the United States. Do some research to find out what was happening. (Clue: It was not a witch-hunt for witches but for people with certain political beliefs.)

4 Do some research about the historical events in Salem in 1692. Note six historical facts which David Calcutt uses in his play. Note any differences between what actually happened and what happens in the play. Think carefully about why the playwright might have made things happen slightly differently in the play.